THE 48 LAWS OF HABIT MASTERY

Break the Cycle, Build Better Habits and Transform Your Life Forever.

I0559370

Victor O. Carl

Printed in the United States of America.

For more information, or to book an event, contact :
(Email & Website)
http://www.48lol.com
mail to : info@48lol.com

Book design by Joseph Campbell
Cover design by C.J (*D reinforced*)

ISBN – Ebook : 978-1-965849-09-5
ISBN - Paperback : 978-1-965849-10-1
ISBN - Hardcover : 978-1-965849-11-8

First Edition : September 2024

CONTENTS

Thank you so much for purchasing my book!

I'm beyond excited to have you as part of my reading community. Your support truly means the world to me.

If you could kindly take a moment to scan the QR code below and share your honest review on Amazon, it would mean so much.

For those reading the ebook version, please click the link:

Amazon Review Link

Your feedback is invaluable—it helps me improve as a writer and strengthens our community. I genuinely love hearing from you and deeply appreciate your thoughts!

Introduction

Wе all have dreams of becoming better versions of ourselves. Maybe it is getting healthier, advancing in your career, nurturing relationships, or simply waking up with a sense of fulfillment. But there is something that often holds us back, this nagging feeling that change is hard, that transformation is elusive.

Many people spend their lives feeling stuck; caught in the same cycles of behavior, wondering why they can't seem to break free and finally achieve what they desire. Here is the truth: the difference between those who realize their full potential and those who do not often boils down to one thing, **HABITS!**

Think about it. What you do on a daily basis shapes the person you are becoming. It is not the grand, sweeping gestures that define us, but the small, often overlooked choices we make each day. In a way, your habits are the building blocks of your life. And while this may seem like a simple idea, mastering your habits is the key to unlocking the life you have always wanted. But how do you go about doing that?

That's what this book is all about.

In **The 48 Laws of Habit Mastery**, I will take you on a journey through the science and art of habit formation. But this will not be just another self-help book filled with generic advice. You will not find vague platitudes like "just stay motivated" or "think positive thoughts." Instead, you will learn specific, actionable strategies grounded in psychology, neuroscience, and real-world examples of people who have successfully mastered their habits to create lasting change.

The Everyday Power of Habits

At its core, a habit is an automatic behavior that is repeated regularly. You likely already have dozens of habits that govern your day without even thinking about them. From the moment you wake up; whether you grab your phone to check emails or take a few deep breaths to prepare for the day; habits are shaping the flow of your life.

The beauty of habits lies in their ability to take something difficult or energy-consuming and turn it into something automatic. Imagine this: if every morning you had to summon all of your willpower to brush your teeth, it would be exhausting. But you do not need to do that, because at some point in your childhood, brushing your teeth became a habit. It requires no thought, no motivation, and no emotional energy. You just do it.

Now imagine if you could take that same automaticity and apply it to habits that serve your deepest goals. Whether it is exercising regularly, being more productive, or cultivating mindfulness, building the right habits can transform your life.

That is what makes this journey exciting. You are not at the mercy of your current habits. You can design the life you want, one habit at a time.

But let us be honest. If creating positive habits were easy, we would all be doing it. There is a reason why so many of us struggle to change. We start strong, full of motivation and excitement, only to lose steam a few days or weeks later. We know what we should do, but for some reason, it just does not stick.

The truth is, we often set ourselves up for failure. We focus on the wrong things; like willpower or motivation; both of which are fleeting. Or we make our habits too complex, thinking that dramatic overhauls will lead to dramatic results.

But here is a secret: **lasting change is built on simplicity**. In "The 48 Laws of Habit Mastery", you will learn that the real key to habit mastery is not about making huge changes overnight. It is about starting small, being consistent, and learning how to adapt your habits to your own unique life.

I present to you a new approach to habit mastery. In this book, you will discover that habits are not just about behavior; they are about identity. Real change happens when you stop focusing solely on your goals and start thinking about the person you want to become. Do you want to be a fit person? A more productive person? Someone who is calm, centered, and focused? The more you align your habits with your identity, the easier they become to maintain. You will not just be trying to "act" healthier; you will see yourself as someone who lives a healthy life, and the actions will follow naturally.

This approach is rooted in the latest scientific research, but it is also deeply human. We are not robots that can be programmed with perfect routines. Life is messy, unpredictable, and full of challenges. That is why the laws you will find in this book are not rigid rules; they are flexible principles designed to adapt to the reality of your everyday life.

You will learn how to start small and build habits that are manageable, yet powerful. You will discover how to design your environment to make success easier and failure harder. You will understand how to use rewards, accountability, and even setbacks to your advantage. And perhaps most importantly, you will learn how to forgive yourself when you slip up, and how to get back on track without guilt or shame.

What you will find in these pages is not a quick fix. Habits, by their very nature, take time to build. But what I can promise you is that if you follow the principles in this book, you will be creating habits that last a lifetime.

Whether your goal is to be more productive, healthier, happier, or more successful, these laws will give you a blueprint for long-term transformation. And it does not matter where you are starting from. You do not need to have all your life together to begin this journey. In fact, the only thing you need is a willingness to start small and stay consistent. Everything else will follow.

As you read through this book, I encourage you to do more than just absorb the information; take action. Start implementing the laws right away, even if it is just one small habit at a time. Pay attention to what works for you and what does not. Reflect, adjust, and keep moving forward. You will find that mastery does not happen all at once; it happens in the small, seemingly insignificant moments when you choose to show up, day after day.

By the end of this book, you will not only have mastered the habits you have always wanted to build; you will have mastered the art of habit formation itself. And that, my friend, is the key to unlocking the life you have always dreamed of.

So, let us begin. Your new life is waiting, one habit at a time.

Law One

Start Small, but Start Now

"Small daily improvements over time lead to stunning results." — *Robin Sharma*

Jerry Seinfeld, one of the most successful comedians of all time, didn't build his career overnight. Early in his career, he realized that the key to improving his craft was not writing perfect jokes, but simply writing consistently. So, he came up with a method to make sure he wrote every single day. Seinfeld hung a large calendar on his wall, and every day he wrote a joke, he would cross off the day with a red X. After a few days, he had a chain of red Xs. His only goal was simple: do not break the chain.

This method of starting small and being consistent, rather than focusing on perfection, helped him hone his skills. Seinfeld did not sit down to write an hour-long comedy special in one go. He focused on just one joke, every day, without fail. Over time, those small, daily efforts compounded into an extraordinary career.

Big changes often seem intimidating. We picture a healthier lifestyle, a more successful career, or a personal transformation, but we never seem to start because the gap between where we are and where we want to be feels too vast. The key to overcoming this inertia lies in starting small. There's incredible power in taking even the tiniest step forward today, rather than waiting for the perfect moment to make a grand gesture. If you want to change your life, the most important decision you can make is to start now, no matter how insignificant the action may seem.

Waiting for the "right" time to start often leads to inaction. You might tell yourself, "I'll begin when the conditions are perfect," but perfection never comes. Life will always have interruptions, distractions, and unforeseen circumstances. By starting small, you bypass the need for ideal conditions and begin building momentum, which is the foundation of all habits.

Let us take fitness as an example. Instead of committing to

running five miles a day when you have never run before, commit to something smaller, like a ten minute walk every morning. It may not seem like much, but the act of getting started rewires your brain to associate progress with action. The simplicity of the task makes it easier to show up each day, and over time, that walk could lead to more significant efforts like running or weight training.

In essence, starting small is about lowering the barrier to entry. It is about tricking yourself into taking the first step by making it so easy that you can't say no. Once you get moving, the momentum builds, and suddenly, the change does not seem so overwhelming.

Practical steps that can help you implement this principle effectively:

- Identify a Micro-Habit: Start by identifying the smallest possible action that moves you in the direction of your desired goal. Think of this as a "micro-habit." For example, if you want to get in shape, your micro-habit could be doing one push-up a day. If you want to start reading more, it could be reading just one page a day. The goal here is to make the habit so small and so easy that there is almost no barrier to starting.

- Set a Clear Time and Place: Habits stick when they are anchored in routine. Pick a specific time and place to do your micro-habit. It could be "right after I wake up,

I'll do one push-up" or "before I go to bed, I'll write 50 words." Setting a clear cue for your habit makes it easier to follow through consistently.

- Focus on Consistency, Not Intensity: At the beginning stages, the key is not how much you do but how often you do it. Focus on showing up consistently and building the habit, rather than worrying about intensity or perfection. Even if you only write a few sentences or do a very short workout, the consistency of action is what will make the habit stick.

- Remove Friction: Make it as easy as possible to start your new habit by removing any obstacles that may prevent you from taking action. This could mean laying out your workout clothes the night before, placing a book on your pillow to remind you to read, or writing down the first sentence of what you want to write the next day.

- Embrace the Power of Starting: Understand that getting started is half the battle. Often, the hardest part of any task is simply beginning. By starting small, you minimize the initial resistance. Once you begin, the momentum often carries you further than you expected.

- Allow Yourself to Grow Slowly: As you master the small habit, allow yourself to grow it incrementally. Once one push-up feels easy, do two. Once one page a day feels effortless, move to two pages. This gradual progression ensures that the habit evolves without overwhelming you, giving you the best chance to sustain it long term.

- Use Visual Reminders: Visual cues can be a powerful motivator for sticking to your habits. Use sticky notes, reminders, or other visual prompts that you will encounter during the day to remind you of the habit you are working on.

- Forgive Missed Days Quickly: Life will happen, and some days you will miss your habit. The key is to forgive yourself quickly and get back on track the next day. Missing one day does not mean failure—it is the pattern of consistency that matters, not perfection.

- Celebrate Small Wins: Do not wait until you have built the perfect habit to celebrate. Celebrate each small win along the way. Reward yourself for each week or month that you have stuck to your new habit, no matter how small it is. This reinforces your behavior and builds positive associations with the habit.

- Reflect on Your Progress Regularly: Make it a point to reflect on how far you have come. Regular reflection helps you stay motivated and reminds you that even small steps are leading to bigger changes. It also gives you the chance to evaluate if you are ready to expand the habit further.

By following these steps, the law that states that, "Start Small, but Start Now" becomes more than just a theory; it becomes actionable advice for anyone looking to build lasting habits. Starting small removes the intimidation factor, and it helps you build momentum, which over time leads to greater and more sustainable success. As you implement these practical steps, you will find that your habits become an integral part of your life, leading to real and lasting change.

Law Two

Make It Easy Before Making It Perfect

"Perfection is not attainable, but if we chase perfection, we can catch excellence." — Vince Lombardi

J ames Clear, the author of Atomic Habits, struggled for years to write consistently. He wanted to be a great writer, but his perfectionist tendencies always held him back. He would spend hours crafting the perfect sentence, paragraph, or idea, only to get stuck in a cycle of self-doubt and procrastination. Eventually, he realized that the problem was not his writing ability; it was his approach.

Clear decided to make writing easier by focusing on quantity rather than quality. He set a goal to write 500 words a day, regardless of whether the writing was good or bad. He embraced the idea that consistency was more important than perfection, and by lowering the standards of what he considered "success," he freed himself to write more often. Over time, his daily writing habit transformed into a career as a bestselling author, with his book selling millions of copies worldwide.

There is a common misconception that in order to build a new habit, you have to do it perfectly right from the start. This belief has held many people back from even attempting something new. But here is the truth; complexity is the enemy of consistency. If your habit feels too difficult or overwhelming, you will struggle to keep it going. The key is to make it easy before you make it perfect.

Perfectionism often leads to paralysis. You might have an ideal vision of how you want things to be, but the more complicated the process, the harder it becomes to sustain. Instead of aiming for perfection right away, start by simplifying the habit as much as possible. This does not mean lowering your standards permanently, but it does mean focusing on consistency first and refinement later.

For example, if you want to build a habit of meditating, do not start by aiming for an hour-long meditation session each day. Instead, commit to five minutes of mindful breathing. Make it so easy that it feels almost impossible not to do it. As you get more comfortable with the habit, you can gradually increase the difficulty and complexity.

This approach works because the hardest part of building any habit is showing up. Once you have shown up consistently for a period of time, it becomes easier to improve the quality of your effort. When the habit is established, you can then shift your focus from doing it easily to doing it well.

Steps To Make It Easy Before Making It Perfect:

- Lower the bar of entry: The biggest obstacle to starting is often the belief that you need to get it right from the beginning. Perfectionism can make tasks seem overwhelming, which leads to procrastination or fear of failure. By lowering the bar of entry, you make it easier to get started. Instead of waiting until conditions are perfect or you feel ready, commit to doing the task in its simplest form. For instance, you can allocate just 10 minutes each day to work on a side project you want to start. This helps you build momentum without the pressure of perfection.

- Embrace the 80% rule: Instead of trying to achieve 100% perfection, aim for 80%. The idea is that getting something done, even if it is not perfect, is better than waiting for the perfect moment that may never come.

Completing tasks at 80% allows you to make meaningful progress while giving you the room to improve and refine over time. When writing an article or report, aim to get your thoughts down without obsessing over every detail. Focus on getting the draft completed first, and then go back later to edit and improve.

- Break Tasks Into Micro-Steps: Breaking larger tasks into smaller, manageable chunks makes it easier to start. Perfectionism tends to make tasks seem bigger than they really are which can lead to paralysis by analysis. By dividing the task into smaller actions, you make it less intimidating, and you can build momentum by completing each small step. Let us say you are writing a book; do not aim to write an entire chapter at once. Break it down into paragraphs, scenes, or even bullet points, focusing on getting one small part done at a time. Or if you want to declutter your home, start with one drawer or one small area rather than trying to tackle the entire house in one go.

- Focus on progress, not perfection: Shift your mindset from achieving perfect results to making steady progress. Every time you take action, even if it is not perfect, you are moving closer to your goal. Perfectionism often robs you of the opportunity to learn and grow because it focuses on the outcome rather than the process. Embrace the idea that each small action is a step forward, even if it is not perfect. Track your progress in a journal or a habit tracker. Note down every time you make progress, no matter how small, and celebrate your efforts rather than focusing on what did not go perfectly.

- Use a time limit to avoid overthinking: One of the most effective ways to beat perfectionism is to give yourself a time limit for completing a task. Setting a timer forces you to act within the time frame rather than spending hours agonizing over details. This approach helps you focus on getting things done rather than making them flawless. Apply this method to any task that you have been procrastinating on, whether it is writing, cleaning, or even decision-making. Limiting your time removes the pressure to be perfect.

- Prioritize learning over perfection: Take mistakes and imperfections as opportunities for learning rather than evidence of failure. Every time you take action, you learn something that helps you improve the next time. Perfectionism prevents action because it fears mistakes. By prioritizing learning, you give yourself permission to try things, make errors, and grow from the experience. After completing a task, spend a few minutes reflecting on what went well and what could be improved. This process helps you build confidence in your ability to learn and adjust, rather than striving for immediate perfection.

- Simplify your tools and resources: Perfectionism often leads people to believe they need the "best" tools, courses, or materials before they can start. However, the more complicated the tools or process, the harder it becomes to take action. Simplifying your resources allows you to focus on the task itself, not the perfection of preparation. If you want to start a new hobby, use basic, readily available tools. For example, if you want to learn photography, start with your phone camera rather than waiting to buy an expensive DSLR.

- Share your work publicly for accountability: One of the biggest drivers of perfectionism is the fear of being judged. By sharing your work or progress publicly, you hold yourself accountable to show up and take action, even when things are not perfect. The fear of judgment decreases as you realize that most people are supportive and more interested in your effort than in your perfection. You can share your progress or results on social media, in a blog, or with a close friend or accountability group. This does not mean sharing only when it is perfect; share the messy parts, too.

- Reward Imperfect Action: It is important to acknowledge and reward yourself for taking imperfect action. When you celebrate the process of taking action, rather than the perfection of the result, you reinforce the habit of starting and progressing. This helps you overcome the paralysis that often comes with chasing perfection. After completing a task, no matter how small or imperfect, reward yourself with something simple. It could be taking a break, enjoying a snack, or doing something you love.

Law Three

Focus on Identity, Not Goals

"You do not rise to the level of your goals. You fall to the level of your systems." — *James Clear*

Michael Phelps did not become the most decorated Olympian in history by focusing solely on winning gold medals. Instead, Phelps and his coach, Bob Bowman, worked on instilling habits that reinforced Phelps's identity as a world-class swimmer. Every day, Phelps followed the same rigorous routine. He visualized his races, went through a series of specific drills, and even practiced how to remain calm in stressful situations, such as when his goggles filled with water during a race.

What set Phelps apart was not just his talent; it was his belief in who he was. He did not think of himself as someone who just swam to win medals; he saw himself as the embodiment of excellence in swimming. His daily habits were not about achieving goals; they were about reinforcing his identity as the best swimmer in the world. The medals were simply a byproduct of who he believed himself to be.

We often think of success in terms of goals. We set a target, like losing weight, making more money, or learning a new skill, and we measure our progress by how close we get to that goal. But what happens when you reach the goal? Does everything magically fall into place, or do you find yourself slipping back into old habits? The reason so many people fail to maintain their success is because they focus too much on the outcome and not enough on the identity behind it.

Habits that stick are identity-based. Instead of asking, "What do I want to achieve?" ask yourself, "Who do I want to become?" When your habits align with your identity, they become automatic and self-sustaining. You are not forcing yourself to act in a certain way; you are acting in accordance with who you believe you are.

Let us say your goal is to read more. You could set a target of reading 50 books a year, but that's focusing on the outcome. A more powerful approach is to focus on becoming a "reader." If you identify as someone who reads every day, the behavior follows naturally. It is no longer about achieving a certain number of books; it is about reinforcing the identity of a reader.

The shift from outcome-based thinking to identity-based thinking is transformative because it changes how you view yourself. Goals are temporary; identity is lasting. If you want lasting change, you need to focus on who you are becoming, not just what you are achieving.

Focusing on identity rather than goals ensures that the changes you make are sustainable because they are rooted in who you are becoming. Goals can be short-lived and outcome-based, often leading to frustration if not achieved within a certain timeframe. But when you focus on identity, you are not chasing a specific result; instead, you are cultivating the habits of the person you want to be. This approach helps to internalize your desired behavior, making it part of your daily life rather than a temporary pursuit.

Moreover, identity-based habits provide more consistency. When you identify as a healthy person, for example, your choices naturally align with that identity, even when you face challenges. You are no longer acting based on external motivations or targets but because these actions reflect who you are. This internal shift ensures that you maintain your habits even after achieving specific goals, as the behavior is now integrated into your sense of self.

Lastly, focusing on identity encourages you to embrace the process rather than fixating on outcomes. This allows for a more patient, long-term approach to growth. The journey becomes about becoming better each day, rather than rushing toward a finish line. As your actions continuously affirm your identity, setbacks are easier to manage because they do not define your self-worth or success. You understand that every action you take is a step toward the person you want to become.

Once Again…

FOCUS ON IDENTITY   NOT GOALS

Law Four

Leverage Your Environment

"The secret of your future is hidden in your daily routine." — *Mike Murdock*

O ur environments are powerful influences, often more so than we realize. While we might think of success or failure in terms of willpower and self-discipline, much of it comes down to the spaces we inhabit. If you want to master your habits, you need to structure your surroundings in ways that support your goals rather than hinder them. Your environment can either act as a catalyst for positive behavior or become a barrier that makes success more difficult to achieve.

Consider how many times you have been distracted at work

because your phone is sitting within arm's reach, or how often you have opted for a snack simply because it was easy to grab. These are examples of how your environment dictates your actions without you even being aware of it. The good news is that by making strategic adjustments to your surroundings, you can make it easier to engage in the habits you want to build while making it harder to indulge in those you are trying to avoid.

One of the most effective ways to encourage good habits is by reducing friction—the effort required to initiate them. Friction is anything that makes it harder to do something, whether it is physical distance, complexity, or inconvenience. When friction is high, we are less likely to perform a behavior; when it is low, the behavior becomes automatic.

For example, if you want to read more, make books more accessible. Place one on your bedside table, in your bag, or at your work desk. If you want to eat healthier, make sure that nutritious foods are within easy reach and prominently displayed, while less healthy options are tucked away or removed from your kitchen altogether. By designing your environment in a way that eliminates friction, you are making it easier for your desired habits to take root.

Another technique is habit stacking, where you link a new habit to an already established one. This method leverages the existing momentum of your environment to facilitate the new habit. For instance, if you already have a habit of making coffee in the morning, stack another habit on top of that, like doing a quick 5-minute meditation while the coffee brews. This way, your environment and your routine support each other in creating lasting change.

Just as you can eliminate friction for good habits, you can also increase it for bad ones. Make the behaviors you want to avoid more difficult to engage in. If you are trying to cut down on social media, delete the apps from your phone or place them in a folder that requires extra effort to access. If you want to reduce TV watching, put the remote control in a different room or unplug the television when you are not using it.

This concept was famously illustrated by the "London Underground experiment," where researchers removed trash cans from a section of the subway to discourage littering. By creating more friction—people had to carry their trash until they found a trash can—the researchers successfully reduced littering by 29%. Similarly, increasing friction for bad habits can drastically decrease how often you engage in them.

Your environment is full of cues that trigger behavior, whether it is the time of day, a place, or an object. By placing visual reminders in strategic locations, you can prompt yourself to engage in good habits more consistently. For example, if you want to drink more water, keep a water bottle on your desk or kitchen counter. If you are trying to develop a morning exercise routine, lay out your workout clothes the night before in a visible spot. These visual cues act as prompts, reminding you to take action when your mind might otherwise be distracted.

Studies show that humans are incredibly responsive to visual stimuli, often more than we are to verbal or mental reminders. By leveraging this to your advantage, you can create an environment that nudges you toward the behaviors you want to cultivate.

Redesigning your environment is not just about removing distractions or setting up cues—it is also about building a support system that nurtures your growth. Surround yourself with people who share your goals or who can hold you accountable for your habits. Social environments, including your home, workplace, and community, can have a profound impact on the habits you form.

Consider joining a group or community that shares your values and ambitions. If you are trying to improve your fitness, for instance, joining a gym where people are actively pursuing the same goal can boost your motivation and adherence to your habits. Similarly, working in a coworking space filled with driven individuals can help reinforce your commitment to productivity.

James Clear, the author of Atomic Habits, struggled early in life with forming productive habits. After suffering a traumatic brain injury in high school, his athletic dreams were shattered. During his recovery, he noticed how small, positive habits transformed his daily life. Clear started adjusting his environment to make these habits easier, whether it was organizing his study materials for easy access or creating a distraction-free zone for work. Over time, these environmental tweaks contributed significantly to his success as a writer, speaker, and entrepreneur. Today, Clear emphasizes that the simplest changes to your environment can yield the most profound results in habit formation.

Your environment will not remain static, and neither should your approach to it. As your goals evolve, so should the spaces you inhabit. Regularly assess your surroundings to ensure they are still aligned with your objectives. Are there new distractions that have crept in? Are your visual cues still effective, or do they need refreshing? Be willing to tweak and adjust your environment to maintain its supportive role in your habit-building journey.

Incorporating habit mastery into your environment is an ongoing process of refinement. What works today might not work tomorrow, and that is okay. The key is to remain adaptable and aware, constantly shaping your environment to serve the person you want to become.

By leveraging your environment, you are not just making it

easier to build good habits, you are creating a space where success is inevitable. With every small change to your surroundings, you are reinforcing the behaviors that define who you are and the life you want to lead.

Law Five

Stack Habits to Build Momentum

"Chains of habit are too light to be felt until they are too heavy to be broken." — Warren Buffett

One of the most effective ways to build and maintain habits is through stacking. Habit stacking is a strategy where you link a new habit to an already established one, making it easier to adopt and stick to. This approach works because it takes advantage of the patterns and routines that are already deeply ingrained in your daily life. By piggybacking a new habit onto something you already do regularly, you are harnessing the power of existing momentum, making the new habit feel more natural and effortless.

For example, if you want to start practicing gratitude, you could link it to your morning coffee routine. Every time you take your first sip, think of one thing you are grateful for. Because you are already in the habit of drinking coffee every morning, the act of gratitude will become easier to incorporate, and over time, the two will become linked in your mind. This way, the new habit of practicing gratitude becomes automatic, flowing naturally from your existing routine.

Once you have successfully stacked one habit onto another, you can continue the process to create a chain of habits. This is where the real power of habit stacking lies: by linking multiple habits together, you build a sequence that feels automatic. This can help you create a highly productive and meaningful routine without feeling overwhelmed.

For instance, let us say you want to develop a stronger morning routine. You could start with an existing habit, like brushing your teeth. From there, you could stack a 10-minute meditation session right after brushing. After meditating, you might decide to do a quick stretch or exercise. Once that's complete, you could journal for five minutes or review your goals for the day. Each habit builds on the previous one, creating a chain of productive behaviors that start your day with momentum.

This method works because it leverages the concept of "cue-response-reward," which is central to habit formation. Each habit acts as a cue for the next, creating a seamless flow that reduces decision fatigue. Over time, this chain of habits becomes second nature, requiring little mental energy to maintain.

Momentum is a critical factor in habit formation. Once you have completed one habit, you are more likely to complete another. This is known as the "domino effect"—small wins lead to bigger ones, and the more success you experience, the more motivated you are to keep going. Habit stacking builds momentum by ensuring that each habit feels effortless and automatic.

Consider how successful people often seem to accomplish so much in their day. The secret is not necessarily that they have more willpower or energy; rather, they've mastered the art of stacking habits to create momentum. Each small task propels them into the next, making it easier to achieve larger goals without burning out.

When you use habit stacking, you are not just building one habit at a time—you are creating a network of behaviors that reinforce each other. As you complete one habit, you gain a sense of accomplishment that motivates you to tackle the next, building momentum throughout your day.

One of the keys to successful habit stacking is starting small. It is tempting to try to overhaul your routine all at once, but this approach often leads to burnout. Instead, focus on linking just one or two small habits to your existing routine. Once those habits become ingrained, you can gradually add more.

For example, if your goal is to improve your fitness, you might start by stacking a habit of doing 10 push-ups right after you wake up in the morning. Once that becomes second nature, you could add a short stretching session or a few minutes of cardio. Over time, these small habits will compound, leading to significant improvements in your fitness without feeling overwhelming.

The key is to ensure that each new habit is manageable and fits naturally into your existing routine. By starting small, you make it easier to maintain consistency, which is essential for long-term success.

In order to successfully stack habits, it is important to identify "anchor habits"—those foundational routines that are already so ingrained in your day that they happen without much thought. These anchor habits can serve as the foundation for your habit stack, acting as reliable cues for the new behaviors you want to add.

Common anchor habits include brushing your teeth, making

coffee, eating lunch, or commuting to work. These activities are part of your daily routine, and because they happen consistently, they provide the perfect opportunity to stack new habits on top of them.

For example, if you want to develop a habit of practicing mindfulness, you might attach it to your daily commute. Every time you get into your car or board public transport, take a few deep breaths and spend a minute focusing on the present moment. By linking mindfulness to a routine task like commuting, you create a habit that feels natural and easy to maintain.

Another important aspect of habit stacking is reinforcing your progress with small rewards. Each time you complete a habit, take a moment to acknowledge your success. This could be as simple as a mental pat on the back or a brief moment of reflection on how far you have come.

Rewards do not need to be extravagant or material. In fact, the most effective rewards are often intrinsic, such as the sense of accomplishment or the positive feelings that come from engaging in a good habit. By rewarding yourself, you strengthen the habit loop, making it more likely that you'll continue to engage in the behavior in the future.

For instance, if you have successfully completed your morning habit stack, reward yourself with a few minutes of relaxation or a small treat. This positive reinforcement helps to cement the habit in your mind, increasing the likelihood that you'll stick with it long-term.

Finally, it is important to recognize that habit stacking is a long-term strategy. Each habit you stack builds on the previous one, creating a compound effect that leads to significant improvements over time. While the results may not be immediate, they will accumulate as you consistently follow through with your habits.

Just as small investments grow over time through compound interest, small habits build momentum and lead to big changes in your life. By stacking habits and creating a routine that flows naturally, you are setting yourself up for long-term success. Each habit may seem small on its own, but when combined with others, the impact can be profound.

Tim Ferriss, author of The 4-Hour Workweek, is known for his obsession with optimization, particularly when it comes to productivity and routines. Like many high performers, Ferriss credits much of his success to the consistency of his daily habits. One strategy he shares is habit stacking, which he used to develop a solid morning routine. By attaching small, productive habits to his existing morning behaviors; such as meditating right after brushing his teeth or journaling immediately after his coffee, he built momentum that carried him through his day. Over time, these small habits compounded, making his mornings not only more productive but also more intentional and calm.

By using habit stacking, you can create a positive feedback loop where each habit reinforces the next, building momentum and making your goals feel easier to achieve. Over time, these habits become second nature, propelling you toward greater productivity, health, and personal growth.

Law Six

Master the Art of Repetition

"We are what we repeatedly do. Excellence, then, is not an act, but a habit." — Aristotle

K obe Bryant, one of the greatest basketball players of all time, is often remembered for his exceptional work ethic. His commitment to practicing the fundamentals of the game set him apart from others, even when he was already considered an elite player. Bryant was known for his dedication to repetition. He would show up for practice at 4:00 a.m., hours before his teammates, to focus on basic drills, like shooting free throws and perfecting footwork.

In his mind, greatness wasn't born from a single heroic effort; it was the result of doing the same thing repeatedly, day in and day out. Bryant once said, "I can't relate to lazy people. We do not speak the same language. I do not understand you. I do not want to understand you." His approach to basketball was simple but profound: master the basics through relentless repetition. Even on days when he didn't feel like practicing, he would push through, knowing that every repetition was a step toward mastery.

His career reflected this mindset. Kobe's five NBA championships, MVP awards, and scoring records were not just results of natural talent—they were the product of thousands of hours of dedicated practice, drilling the same moves over and over again. The lesson Kobe Bryant left us is clear: repetition breeds mastery, and mastery breeds greatness.

Repetition is at the core of habit formation. Whether you want to develop a new skill, break an old habit, or reinforce a positive behavior, repetition is the vehicle that gets you there. Every time you repeat an action, you strengthen the neural pathways in your brain associated with that behavior. This process, known as "neuroplasticity," enables your brain to rewire itself, making the behavior easier to perform over time.

When we talk about the importance of repetition, we're not just referring to mechanical repetition, but deliberate, intentional practice. It is not about going through the motions but about focusing on improvement with each attempt. This is why consistent repetition is so powerful—it allows you to make incremental progress, and over time, those small gains add up to substantial improvements.

Think of your brain like a muscle: the more you use it in a

certain way, the stronger it becomes. If you want to develop a habit of waking up early, for example, the more days you force yourself to wake up at the same time, the easier it becomes. Your brain starts to expect that behavior, and soon enough, waking up early feels natural, rather than a struggle.

One of the biggest challenges in mastering repetition is overcoming what is known as the "plateau of latent potential." This is the phase where you are putting in the work, but it feels like you are not making progress. It is the point at which many people give up, assuming their efforts are in vain. But in reality, it is just the nature of growth and change.

Progress often happens below the surface, in small, almost imperceptible ways. Just like bamboo plants, which spend years developing strong roots underground before they suddenly shoot up into the air, your efforts are laying the groundwork for future success, even if you can't see immediate results.

To master the art of repetition, you have to push through the plateau. This is where most people fail, and it is what separates those who achieve mastery from those who do not. Understand that the results will come if you keep putting in the effort. Each repetition is a brick in the wall, even if the wall hasn't taken shape yet.

One common misconception about habit formation is that

intensity matters more than consistency. In reality, it is far better to practice small habits consistently than to push yourself too hard in short bursts. Let us say you want to build a habit of exercising. Many people make the mistake of going all out for the first few days, only to burn out and quit within a week. It is much more effective to start with a manageable routine—something as simple as 15 minutes of exercise every day—than to try to overhaul your life overnight.

You reduce the mental resistance to performing the habit by focusing on small, repeatable actions. Consistency is key here. It is not about how intensely you can practice a habit in one go, but how often you can repeat it. This approach aligns with the concept of "compound interest," where small investments over time yield massive returns. In the case of habits, every repetition you complete adds to your investment in the new behavior.

To master repetition, it is important to make your habits a seamless part of your daily routine. The more friction you remove from performing the habit, the more likely you are to stick with it. This is where strategies like habit stacking and environment design come into play.

By stacking new habits onto existing ones, you create a natural trigger for the behavior you want to repeat. For example, if you want to develop a habit of reading every day, you might attach that habit to something you already do, like having your morning coffee. By pairing the two activities, you create a chain of events that makes it easier to complete the new habit.

Similarly, you can leverage your environment to encourage repetition. If your goal is to write every day, make sure your workspace is set up for success. Keep your writing tools readily available, create a distraction-free zone, and designate a specific time each day for the task. The easier it is to perform the habit, the less likely you are to skip it.

Many people rely on motivation to maintain their habits, but the truth is, motivation is fleeting. There will be days when you do not feel motivated to work out, study, or practice your new skill. That's where the power of repetition becomes invaluable. By repeating an action often enough, it becomes ingrained in your routine, requiring less willpower to maintain.

In fact, the more you rely on motivation, the more likely you are to fail. Motivation fluctuates, but habits rooted in repetition persist. When Kobe Bryant woke up at 4:00 a.m. to practice, he wasn't relying on motivation. He was relying on discipline, which was built through years of repeating the same actions over and over, even when he didn't feel like it.

The goal should be to make your habits so automatic that you do them regardless of how you feel at the moment. Repetition is the mechanism that makes this possible.

Mastery through repetition requires embracing the boring work. This is the grind, the unglamorous side of greatness that most people do not see. It is the hours spent practicing free throws, writing drafts, or running drills. It is easy to get excited about a new habit at the beginning, but the real test comes when the excitement fades, and you are left with nothing but the routine.

Success doesn't come from doing extraordinary things once; it comes from doing ordinary things extraordinarily well, over and over again. This is why repetition is so critical—it trains you to focus on the process rather than the outcome. Instead of chasing instant results, you learn to trust that the process will eventually lead to the success you are after.

Repetition is the invisible thread that ties all habits together. Whether you are aiming to improve your health, learn a new skill, or achieve a personal goal, repetition is the key to making it happen. It is not glamorous, and it is not always exciting, but it is the surest path to success.

You are committing to the long game by committing to repetition. You are acknowledging that greatness is not born from single acts of heroism but from the daily grind of showing up and putting in the work. Each repetition strengthens the habit, builds momentum, and brings you one step closer to mastery.

Law Seven

Reward Consistency, Not Perfection

"It is not about being perfect. It is about effort. And when you bring that effort every single day, that's where transformation happens. That's how change occurs." — *Jillian Michaels*

Perfectionism is one of the most common barriers to habit mastery. The desire to get everything "just right" can paralyze action, making it difficult to start or continue with any endeavor. Whether it is writing, exercising, or working on a project, the quest for perfection can lead to procrastination, self-doubt, and eventually, burnout.

People often set lofty expectations for themselves, thinking that they must perform at their best every single time. However, this mindset can be crippling because it focuses on outcomes rather than the process. The problem with perfectionism is that it doesn't account for the fact that life is messy and unpredictable. There will always be days when conditions aren't ideal, when motivation is low, or when you are simply not at your best.

The solution? Shift your focus from perfection to consistency. Consistency is far more achievable, sustainable, and rewarding in the long run. When you prioritize consistency, you are not aiming to be perfect every time. Instead, you are committing to showing up, regardless of the circumstances. This approach not only lowers the pressure but also builds resilience, which is essential for long-term success.

One of the most powerful ways to reinforce the habit of consistency is to celebrate the act of showing up. When you reward yourself for simply doing the habit, even if it is not done perfectly, you reinforce the behavior and make it more likely to stick. This concept aligns with the idea of "identity-based habits," where the focus is on becoming the kind of person who shows up, rather than on achieving a specific outcome.

For example, if you are trying to build a habit of going to the gym, do not focus on having the perfect workout every time. Instead, celebrate the fact that you made it to the gym, even if all you did was 10 minutes on the treadmill. The mere act of showing up reinforces your identity as someone who prioritizes fitness, and over time, those small, consistent actions compound into meaningful progress.

Rewarding consistency doesn't have to be complicated. It can be as simple as giving yourself a mental pat on the back or tracking your progress with a habit tracker. The key is to shift your mindset from "I must do this perfectly" to "I showed up, and that's what matters." This change in perspective not only makes habit formation more enjoyable but also reduces the pressure to be perfect, which can be a significant roadblock to progress.

When you prioritize consistency over perfection, you tap into the power of compounding. Compounding is the idea that small, repeated actions lead to exponential results over time. This concept applies not only to finance but also to habits and personal development.

Imagine someone who practices guitar for 10 minutes every day versus someone who practices for an hour but only once a week. Over time, the person who practices daily, even for a short duration, will make more progress than the person who practices sporadically, even if their sessions are longer. The key is the consistency, not the intensity or perfection of each practice session.

The same principle applies to any habit you want to develop. Whether it is writing, learning a new language, or exercising, the small, consistent efforts you make each day will add up in ways that might not be immediately noticeable but will have a profound impact in the long term. By focusing on consistency, you remove the need for each session to be perfect, allowing the habit to grow naturally and sustainably.

Perfectionism can be particularly harmful because it creates an all-or-nothing mindset. If you believe that every effort must be perfect, you are more likely to give up when things do not go as planned. This is why so many people abandon their goals after a minor setback—they feel that they've already failed, so why bother continuing?

Consistency, on the other hand, embraces the idea that progress is non-linear. There will be good days and bad days, but what matters is that you keep going. When you accept that not every attempt will be perfect, you free yourself from the fear of failure and make it easier to recover from setbacks.

For example, let us say you have set a goal to write 500 words every day. On some days, you might write 1,000 words, while on others, you might struggle to hit 300. Perfectionism would make you feel like a failure on the days when you didn't meet your goal, which could lead to frustration and eventually giving up. But if you focus on consistency, you'll recognize that even writing 300 words is progress, and that showing up is what really matters.

A powerful way to build consistency is by understanding and utilizing habit loops. A habit loop consists of a cue, a routine, and a reward. The cue triggers the behavior, the routine is the action you take, and the reward reinforces the behavior, making it more likely to be repeated. You can make it easier to maintain your habits over the long term by designing habit loops that reward consistency rather than perfection.

For instance, if you are trying to build a habit of going for a run every morning, the cue might be placing your running shoes by your bed the night before. The routine is going for the run, and the reward could be something as simple as enjoying a post-run cup of coffee or marking off the day on a habit tracker. By focusing on the consistency of completing the loop rather than on the quality or duration of the run, you reinforce the habit in a way that feels achievable and sustainable.

One of the greatest benefits of focusing on consistency over perfection is that it builds resilience. When you accept that you do not need to be perfect, you are less likely to give up in the face of setbacks. This resilience is crucial because no matter how committed you are to your habits, there will be obstacles along the way. Life gets busy, motivation wanes, and unexpected challenges arise.

However, if you have built the habit of showing up consistently, you'll have the resilience to push through these challenges. You won't see a missed day or an imperfect effort as a failure but rather as a natural part of the process. This mindset shift allows you to stay on track, even when things do not go as planned.

In the journey toward habit mastery, consistency will always outlast perfectionism. When you reward consistency, you create a sustainable foundation for growth, resilience, and long-term success. Remember, it is not about being perfect every day—it is about showing up and putting in the effort, no matter how small. Over time, these small, consistent actions will lead to extraordinary results, far surpassing the fleeting satisfaction of perfection.

James Clear, author of Atomic Habits, is one of the leading voices in habit formation today. However, his journey to mastery wasn't built on perfection. Instead, Clear embraced the power of small, consistent actions. Early in his career, Clear committed to writing one article every Monday and Thursday, no matter what. He didn't demand that every article be perfect—just that it was written and shared with his audience.

Some of the articles were fantastic; others weren't. But by staying consistent, Clear built a body of work that attracted millions of readers. Today, his writing has been read by millions, and his book, Atomic Habits, has become a global bestseller. Clear's success didn't come from waiting for inspiration or striving for perfection. It came from showing up and putting in the work, even when he didn't feel like it.

This approach—rewarding consistency over perfection—helped Clear build a successful writing career, reinforcing that the habit of consistently showing up is far more powerful than waiting for the perfect moment.

The key to building lasting habits is not to aim for perfection but to embrace the process of showing up consistently, celebrating the small wins, and trusting that progress will follow.

Once Again…

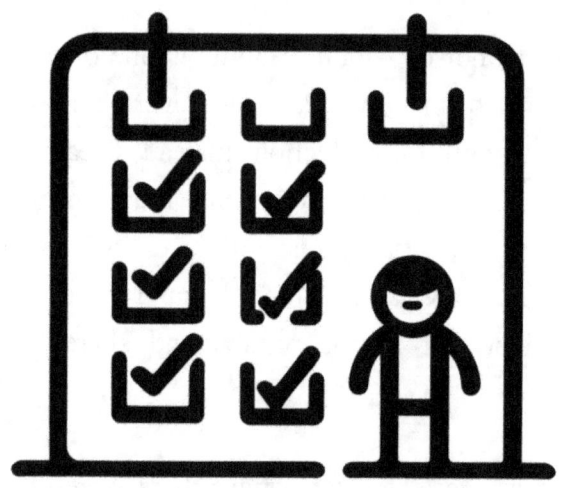

REWARD CONSISTENCY
NOT PERFECTION.

Law Eight

Know When to Break the Pattern

"The definition of insanity is doing the same thing over and over again, but expecting different results." — Albert Einstein

Habits are incredibly powerful tools for personal and professional growth, but they can also become limiting if we cling to them when they no longer serve their purpose. It is easy to fall into the trap of continuing a habit simply because it is comfortable or familiar. After all, habits are designed to remove the need for constant decision-making; they make life easier by automating certain behaviors. However, when a habit no longer contributes to your growth, sticking to it can become counterproductive, even destructive.

Stubbornly adhering to a routine that no longer benefits you can lead to stagnation. It is like trying to drive forward while keeping one foot on the brake. Sure, you are moving, but you are also holding yourself back from reaching your full potential. This is especially true in a fast-paced world where circumstances, goals, and personal values are constantly evolving.

The key to avoiding this trap is awareness. You must develop the ability to regularly assess whether your habits are still aligned with your current objectives and needs. This requires a willingness to be honest with yourself and to accept that what worked before may not work now. Breaking a pattern is not about failure—it is about adaptability and growth.

How do you know when it is time to break a habit or routine? The first step is to pay attention to your results. If a habit that once contributed to your success or well-being is now causing frustration, burnout, or diminishing returns, it is time to reconsider its role in your life. This could manifest in different ways:

- Physical and emotional fatigue: If a habit is draining your energy rather than recharging you, it is a sign that it may no longer be serving you. For example, a daily workout routine that once energized you might now feel like a chore that leaves you exhausted. This could indicate that your body needs a different approach, such as a change in intensity or focus.

- Lack of progress: If you have been following a habit for a while and aren't seeing the results you once did, it is worth evaluating whether the habit needs to evolve. Perhaps you have hit a plateau in your learning or development because the habit has become too comfortable. In such cases, it may be time to push yourself out of your comfort zone by trying something new.

- Changing goals: As you grow and evolve, your goals may change. A habit that once supported a specific goal may no longer be relevant if your priorities have shifted. For instance, a habit of reading business books might have been useful when you were focused on career growth, but if you are now more interested in personal development or creativity, that habit may need to be replaced with something more aligned with your new direction.

The important thing is to remain flexible. Habits are tools, not rules. They're meant to serve your goals, not to become rigid frameworks that limit your growth. Being open to change allows you to adapt to new challenges and opportunities, making it easier to thrive in an ever-changing world.

Breaking a habit, especially one that's been ingrained for a long time, can be uncomfortable. Humans are creatures of habit for a reason—our brains are wired to conserve energy, and habits provide a way to automate behaviors so we can focus on more complex tasks. But when a habit no longer serves its purpose, holding onto it can be detrimental to your progress.

It takes courage to break a pattern. This courage comes from trusting that change, even when uncomfortable, can lead to greater growth. It is about acknowledging that sticking to a routine out of sheer stubbornness is not the same as discipline.

Discipline is about making choices that align with your goals and values, even when they're hard. Stubbornness, on the other hand, is about resisting change because it feels safe or familiar.

To develop the courage to break patterns, you need to shift your mindset from one of fear to one of opportunity. Ask yourself, "What's the worst that could happen if I let go of this habit? What's the best that could happen if I replace it with something better?" Often, the fear of breaking a habit is based on an imagined loss of security or control, but the reality is that letting go of outdated routines can open up new possibilities for growth and achievement.

Breaking a pattern doesn't mean abandoning habits altogether—it means evolving them to better serve your current needs. This could mean tweaking an existing habit, replacing it with a new one, or even temporarily letting go of a routine to give yourself space to explore new options.

For example, let us say you have built a habit of working on a side project for an hour every evening. At first, this habit was highly productive and helped you make significant progress. But now, after months of following the same routine, you feel burnt out, and your enthusiasm for the project has dwindled. Rather than forcing yourself to continue with the habit, you might consider scaling it back to 30 minutes or taking a short break to recharge your creativity.

By evolving your habits in this way, you prevent burnout and maintain the energy needed for long-term success. You also ensure that your habits remain aligned with your goals, which will naturally evolve over time as you grow and change.

Sometimes, the best decision is to abandon a habit entirely. This is particularly true when a habit is tied to a goal that's no longer relevant or when it is actively harming your well-being. For example, if you have developed a habit of working late into the night to meet a deadline, but that habit is affecting your health and relationships, it is time to reconsider whether the habit is worth maintaining.

Abandoning a habit doesn't mean you have failed—it means you have recognized that your priorities have changed. By letting go of the habit, you create space for new routines that better support your current needs and values.

Habits are powerful tools for personal growth, but they are not meant to be rigid. The true power of habits lies in their ability to evolve alongside you. Knowing when to break the pattern, adapt, or abandon a habit altogether is essential for sustained growth and success. Remember, stubbornness in habits can be as destructive as inconsistency. The key is to remain flexible, to continually assess whether your habits are serving your current goals, and to have the courage to let go when necessary. By embracing change and adapting your habits, you ensure that they remain a force for good in your life, driving you toward continued growth and success.

Steve Jobs, the visionary behind Apple, was known for his dedication to innovation and simplicity. However, what's less known is how often he was willing to break his own patterns and habits when they no longer served his vision or the company. One of the most famous examples of this was when Jobs made the difficult decision to discontinue the iPod, the product that had revolutionized Apple and brought it back from the brink of collapse.

At the time, the iPod was Apple's most successful product, dominating the portable music player market. Yet, Jobs saw the future—smartphones were quickly becoming all-in-one devices, and the iPod's popularity would inevitably wane. Despite the iPod's continued success, Jobs wasn't afraid to disrupt its growth, shifting the company's focus to the iPhone, which would go on to change the world.

This ability to break the pattern, to recognize when a habit or pattern no longer serves its original purpose, was one of the key reasons for Jobs' sustained success. It wasn't about being stubbornly attached to a habit or tradition but about knowing when to let go and evolve. His willingness to abandon the iPod at its peak in favor of something even greater is a perfect example of how breaking a pattern can lead to unprecedented growth.

Once Again...

KNOW WHEN TO BREAK THE PATTERN.

Law Nine

Track Your Progress Religiously

"What gets measured, gets managed." — Peter Drucker

Jerry Seinfeld, one of the most successful comedians of all time, is known not only for his humor but also for his disciplined approach to writing jokes. Early in his career, Seinfeld committed to writing jokes every single day, no matter what. His method for staying consistent was simple yet powerful: he used a large wall calendar and placed a big red

"X" over each day that he completed his writing task. As the Xs accumulated, Seinfeld created a chain of successful days. The goal was to never break the chain.

This visual tracking system helped Seinfeld stay motivated, even on days when he didn't feel like writing. By measuring his progress and reinforcing it with a visual reminder, Seinfeld built a habit that contributed to his success as a comedian. This method, now known as "do not Break the Chain," has been adopted by countless people looking to build lasting habits in various areas of life.

Seinfeld's story illustrates the power of tracking progress. Whether you are writing jokes, building a fitness routine, or working toward personal growth, measuring your progress can provide the motivation needed to keep going, even when motivation wanes.

Tracking your progress is a crucial element in habit formation. It serves multiple purposes, from holding yourself accountable to providing motivation when the initial excitement of starting a new habit wears off. When you track your progress, you make the abstract—your goals and habits—tangible. It is no longer just an idea or intention in your mind but something real, visible, and measurable.

Research has shown that people who monitor their progress are more likely to achieve their goals than those who do not.

Tracking gives you data that you can use to evaluate your progress, make adjustments, and celebrate small wins along the way. Without this feedback loop, it is easy to lose sight of how far you have come and get discouraged.

Let us break down why tracking your progress is so essential:

- Accountability: When you measure your actions, you hold yourself accountable. A habit tracker or journal creates a sense of responsibility, reminding you that the habit is something you have committed to. The simple act of recording whether you have followed through with your habit for the day can push you to be more consistent.

- Motivation: Progress can be slow, and it is easy to feel like you are not getting anywhere. But tracking your actions allows you to see how far you have come. Each small win, each day of success, adds up. This visual representation of your progress provides motivation to keep going, even on tough days.

- Feedback and Adjustment: Tracking gives you the data you need to evaluate your performance. If you notice that you are struggling to stick to a habit, you can analyze the data and make adjustments. Maybe the habit needs to be broken down into smaller steps, or perhaps your environment is not supportive. Whatever the issue, tracking helps you identify it and make necessary changes.

- Celebration: Celebrating small wins is crucial for maintaining motivation. When you track your progress, you have concrete milestones to celebrate. Whether it is completing a full week of workouts, sticking to a morning routine, or consistently writing in your journal, these moments of success reinforce the habit and keep you moving forward.

There are several ways to track your habits and progress. The key is to find a method that works best for you and that you'll actually stick with. Here are a few popular methods to consider:

- Habit Tracker (Paper or Digital): A habit tracker is a simple but effective tool for tracking daily habits. You can use a physical journal, a printed calendar, or a digital app. Every day that you complete your habit, you mark it off. Over time, this creates a visual chain of success, much like Seinfeld's "do not Break the Chain" method.

- Journaling: Writing about your habits and progress in a journal allows for deeper reflection. You can use a journal to note not only whether you completed your habit but also how you felt, any challenges you faced, and what worked well. This type of tracking provides more qualitative data and can help you gain insights into your behavior.

- Spreadsheets: For those who love data and numbers, tracking habits in a spreadsheet can be incredibly satisfying. You can log the days you completed a habit, calculate success rates, and even create graphs to visualize your progress over time.

- Apps: There are numerous habit-tracking apps available that can make tracking convenient and accessible. Many of these apps allow you to set reminders, track multiple habits, and see your progress in real time.

No matter which method you choose, the key is consistency. Make tracking a part of your daily or weekly routine, just like the habit you are trying to build.

If you are new to habit tracking, it is essential to keep things simple at the beginning. Start by choosing one or two key habits that you want to focus on, and decide how you'll track them. Here is a step-by-step guide to help you get started:

- Choose a Habit to Track: Identify the habit you want to build. It could be anything from exercising, reading, meditating, or drinking more water. Make sure the habit is specific and measurable.

- Pick Your Tracking Method: Decide whether you'll use a paper habit tracker, a digital app, or a journal to track your progress. Choose the method that feels most natural and motivating for you.

- Set a Time Frame: Decide how long you'll track the habit before evaluating your progress. A common time frame is 30 days, but you can adjust this based on the complexity of the habit.

- Make Tracking Part of Your Routine: Set a specific time each day to update your habit tracker. It could be first thing in the morning, right before bed, or during your lunch break. The key is to make tracking as automatic as the habit itself.

- Review and Adjust: At the end of your chosen time frame, review your progress. Have you been consistent? Did you face any obstacles? Use this data to make adjustments to your habit or tracking method as needed.

When tracking your habits, it is essential to focus on progress, not perfection. It is easy to get discouraged if you miss a day or have a setback. But the point of tracking is not to be perfect—it is to stay consistent over the long term. As long as you are showing up more often than not, you are moving in the right direction.

For example, if your goal is to meditate for 10 minutes every day and you end up missing two days out of the week, do not beat yourself up. Celebrate the five days you meditated and focus on getting back on track. The more you celebrate small wins, the more motivated you'll be to continue.

Remember that habit formation is a marathon, not a sprint. The ultimate goal is consistency, and tracking your progress helps you build that consistency over time.

The act of tracking taps into a powerful psychological principle, The Hawthorne Effect. This effect states that individuals modify their behavior in response to being observed or measured. When you track your habits, you essentially become the observer of your own behavior. Knowing that you'll be recording your actions can make you more mindful and intentional about sticking to your habit.

Additionally, tracking creates a feedback loop that reinforces the habit. Each time you mark off a day, you receive a small hit of dopamine, the brain's "reward" chemical. This positive reinforcement strengthens the neural pathways associated with the habit, making it easier to repeat over time.

Tracking your progress is not just about staying accountable. It is about leveraging the compounding effect of small, consistent actions. Each day you track your habit, you are building momentum and reinforcing your commitment to personal growth. Whether you are using a simple habit tracker, a detailed journal, or a digital app, the key is to stay consistent and focus on progress, not perfection.

As Jerry Seinfeld demonstrated with his "do not Break the Chain" method, tracking can be the difference between success and stagnation. By measuring your actions, you give yourself the tools to stay motivated, make adjustments, and celebrate the small wins that lead to long-term success.

So, whatever your goals may be, start tracking today and watch how it transforms your habits and your life.

Law Ten

Make Bad Habits Invisible

"Out of sight, out of mind." — Ancient Proverb

In a fascinating study conducted by Brian Wansink, a professor at Cornell University, the power of visibility on eating habits was explored. Wansink wanted to understand how our environment affects how much we eat, and he found that when people were presented with food that was easily accessible and visible, they were much more likely to eat it, even when they were not hungry.

In one of his experiments, he placed candy in two different jars in office spaces: one jar was transparent, and the other was opaque. The candy in the transparent jar was eaten much faster and in greater quantities than the candy in the opaque jar. Why? Because when people saw the candy, it triggered their craving. However, when the candy was hidden from sight, people were less likely to think about it, and as a result, they ate less.

Wansink's work underscores a simple truth: we are more likely to engage in behaviors that are cued by our environment. The more accessible or visible a temptation is, the more likely we are to give in to it. Conversely, when we make bad habits invisible or remove the cues that trigger them, we significantly reduce the likelihood of engaging in those behaviors.

Bad habits often begin with a simple trigger; something that reminds you or prompts you to take a specific action. These triggers, or environmental cues, can range from visual stimuli (seeing junk food on the counter) to emotional states (feeling stressed and reaching for a cigarette). What's important to realize is that many of these triggers operate unconsciously. You might not even be aware that your environment is nudging you toward behaviors that do not serve your best interests.

In his book Atomic Habits, James Clear explains that one of the most effective ways to break a bad habit is to make it invisible. This means eliminating or minimizing the triggers in your environment that lead you to engage in the behavior. When you reduce the visibility or accessibility of a bad habit, you are far less likely to act on it. The key idea is that if you do not see the cue, the behavior doesn't get triggered.

Clear provides an example of this with his own life. To reduce his screen time, he began keeping his phone in another room while working. By making the phone invisible and less accessible, he reduced the temptation to check it constantly. This simple adjustment allowed him to stay focused and avoid the bad habit of mindlessly scrolling through apps.

Making bad habits invisible is one of the most powerful ways to reduce or eliminate them. It doesn't require willpower or motivation; it simply relies on restructuring your environment to remove the cues that trigger the habit. Here is how you can do it:

Identify the Triggers. Before you can make a bad habit invisible, you need to identify what triggers it. Triggers can be visual, emotional, social, or even related to time or location. For example:

- Visual triggers. You see junk food on the counter, and you feel the urge to eat it.
- Emotional triggers: You feel stressed, so you reach for a cigarette or junk food.
- Social triggers: You spend time with certain friends who encourage unhealthy habits.
- Time/Location triggers: You might have a habit of snacking late at night or procrastinating when working in a specific room.

Once you have identified the cues that trigger your bad habit, you can work on removing or reducing their presence in your environment.

Remove Visual Cues. The simplest way to make a bad habit invisible is to remove the visual cues that trigger it. Visual cues are powerful because they immediately grab your attention and initiate a craving or behavior. Here are some examples:

- Junk Food: If you want to stop eating junk food, do not leave it out in the open. Put it in a cabinet where you won't see it, or better yet, do not buy it in the first place. Stock your kitchen with healthier options, and make those more visible and accessible.
- Phone Distraction: If you are trying to focus and find yourself constantly checking your phone, leave it in another room or put it on "Do Not Disturb" mode. If you do not see or hear notifications, you won't be tempted to check your phone.
- Social Media: If you want to cut back on social media use, delete the apps from your phone or log out of your accounts after each session. The more steps it takes to access the platform, the less likely you'll mindlessly scroll through it.

Restructure Your Environment. In addition to removing visual cues, you can make bad habits more difficult by restructuring your environment in a way that reduces the chances of engaging in them. For instance:

- Work Environment: If you want to be more productive and avoid distractions, create a workspace that is free of unnecessary gadgets or items that lead to procrastination. Have only the tools you need for work in your immediate vicinity.
- Evening Routines: If you are trying to get to bed earlier, set up your bedroom in a way that encourages winding down. Keep screens out of the room, lower the lights, and set a specific time to turn off electronics.
- Fitness: If you want to exercise more often, make your workout clothes and equipment easily accessible.

Place your gym bag by the door or your workout shoes where you can see them. Conversely, if you are trying to avoid late-night snacking, keep unhealthy food far away from easy reach, such as in the garage or a high cabinet.

Reduce Social Cues. Bad habits are often reinforced by social environments. You may have certain friends or colleagues who influence your behavior negatively, whether it is by encouraging unhealthy eating, smoking, or engaging in gossip. While it is not always possible to avoid these social situations, you can limit your exposure:

- Distance Yourself from Negative Influences: If certain people trigger your bad habits, reduce the amount of time you spend with them or suggest healthier alternatives when you do hang out.
- Seek Positive Reinforcement: Surround yourself with people who encourage the behaviors you want to cultivate. If you are trying to build healthier habits, spend more time with friends who share those goals.

Another critical aspect of making bad habits invisible is reducing their accessibility. The more difficult it is to engage in a bad habit, the less likely you are to follow through. A study conducted at Google showed how changing accessibility could influence behavior. In one office, Google made small tweaks to encourage healthier choices, like putting bottled water in convenient locations while placing sugary drinks further away. As a result, employees drank significantly more water and fewer sodas simply because the healthier option was easier to access.

You can apply the same strategy to your own life and business; it works like a charm.

While making bad habits invisible is essential, it is equally important to make good habits more visible. The more you expose yourself to positive cues, the more likely you are to engage in behaviors that align with your goals.

Your environment plays a pivotal role in shaping your habits, for better or worse. By making bad habits invisible and good habits more visible, you create an environment that supports your goals and reduces the chances of engaging in behaviors that hold you back.

The power to change your habits lies not only within you but also in the world around you. Take control of your surroundings, and let them work for you, not against you.

Once Again…

MAKE BAD HABITS INVISIBLE

Law Eleven

Never Let a Missed Day Become Two

"Success is the sum of small efforts, repeated day in and day out." — Robert Collier

Jerry Seinfeld, the renowned comedian, credits his success and productivity to a simple yet powerful system: never break the chain. Early in his career, Seinfeld developed the habit of writing jokes every single day. To keep himself accountable, he used a large wall calendar, and every day that he wrote, he marked a big red "X" over that day. The goal? Do not break the chain.

Seinfeld's method focused on consistency rather than perfection. He knew that some days he wouldn't write great jokes, but it wasn't about quality—it was about showing up, every day, no matter what. The beauty of this system is that even if he missed one day, he would immediately get back on track the next day, ensuring that a single missed day didn't turn into a series of missed opportunities.

This simple visual system helped Seinfeld build momentum and maintain his habit over time. It is a principle that applies to all areas of life: the power of habits lies not in perfection but in persistence. Missing a day is not a failure; it is what happens after that matters.

When building habits, momentum is everything. Each day that you follow through on your habit, you strengthen the neural pathways that make that behavior automatic. Think of it like pushing a heavy ball up a hill. At first, it takes a tremendous amount of effort to get the ball rolling, but once it starts moving, it becomes easier and easier to keep it going. That's the power of momentum.

However, missing a day can feel like letting go of that ball. When you miss one day, the ball starts to slow down. If you miss two days in a row, it can stop altogether and getting it moving again requires even more effort than before.

This is why it is so important to never let a missed day turn into two. Missing one day is not the end of the world, and in fact, it is entirely normal. Life happens. You might get sick, have an unusually busy day, or just feel unmotivated. But the difference between success and failure in habit formation often comes down to how quickly you get back on track.

The secret to habit mastery is not in never slipping up, it is in making sure that when you do, you recover quickly. A single missed day is just a bump in the road, but two missed days can become the start of a downward spiral.

Steps to Recovering Quickly After Missing a Day

Acknowledge, do not Dwell: When you miss a day, the first thing to do is acknowledge it, but do not dwell on it. Feeling guilty or frustrated with yourself won't help. Instead, recognize that a slip is part of the process and remind yourself that missing one day won't undo all of your progress.

Identify What Went Wrong: Take a moment to reflect on why you missed the day. Was it because of circumstances outside your control, like an emergency or unexpected event? Or was it due to procrastination, lack of motivation, or poor planning? Understanding why you missed a day can help you prevent it from happening again.

For example, if you missed a workout because you didn't set aside time in your schedule, you can plan ahead next time by blocking off time for exercise. If you skipped a healthy meal because you didn't have the right ingredients, you can prepare your meals in advance to avoid the same issue.

Recommit to the Habit: After missing a day, the most important step is to recommit to your habit as soon as possible. Do not wait for the "perfect" time to start again. The next day is your opportunity to get back on track. The longer you wait, the harder it becomes to restart.

Remind yourself why you started the habit in the first place: What are the benefits you are aiming for? Whether it is better health, increased productivity, or personal growth, reconnecting with your motivation will help you refocus and recommit to the habit.

Lower the Barrier for Success: On the day after a missed habit, lower the barrier to success. If you missed your workout, for instance, do not try to make up for it by doing an extra-long session the next day. Instead, start small. Do a 10-minute workout to get back into the routine. The goal is to re-establish the habit of showing up, not to punish yourself for missing a day.

Similarly, if you missed a day of writing, do not force yourself to write a full chapter the next day. Start with a single paragraph or even a sentence. Once you have overcome the initial resistance, you'll find it easier to continue.

Use Visual Reminders Visual reminders, like Jerry Seinfeld's productivity chain, can be powerful motivators to stay consistent. Use a habit tracker, calendar, or journal to mark each day that you follow through on your habit. The satisfaction of seeing a long streak of consistent behavior will motivate you to avoid breaking the chain.

When you miss a day, your goal should be to quickly re-establish that streak. Rather than focusing on the missed day, focus on how quickly you can build momentum again.

One of the biggest obstacles to habit mastery is "all-or-nothing" thinking. This mindset tells you that if you can't do something perfectly, it is not worth doing at all. If you miss one day, this mindset might trick you into thinking that your entire effort has been wasted and that there's no point in continuing.

In reality, this is far from the truth. Progress is not linear, and setbacks are a normal part of the journey. The key is to avoid letting a small slip derail your entire effort. One missed day doesn't mean you have failed—it just means you are human.

Instead of striving for perfection, strive for consistency. The goal is not "to never miss a day"; the goal is to stay on track over the long term. By shifting your focus from perfection to progress, you allow yourself the flexibility to recover from setbacks and continue moving forward.

Habit formation is not just about discipline; it is about resilience. The ability to bounce back after a missed day is a critical skill that separates those who succeed in mastering their habits from those who do not. Resilience means accepting that setbacks will happen, but they do not have to define your journey.

Each time you recover from a missed day, you strengthen your mental toughness and resilience. You prove to yourself that a single mistake doesn't have the power to derail your progress unless you let it. Over time, this resilience becomes a core part of your identity, and you become someone who can navigate obstacles and stay committed to your goals.

The secret to lasting habit mastery is not in never missing a day—it is in how quickly you recover when you do. Momentum is fragile, but it is also renewable. Missing one day won't break your progress, but missing two days can. The key is to avoid letting a single slip turn into a series of missed opportunities.

You can quickly get back on track by acknowledging the missed day, reflecting on what went wrong, and recommitting to your habit. Lower the barrier for success, use visual reminders, and cultivate resilience. Remember, the goal is consistency over perfection. Each day you show up, you are reinforcing the habit and moving closer to mastery.

Once Again...

Never let a missed day become two.

Law Twelve

Surround Yourself with Habit Builders

"You are the average of the five people you spend the most time with." — Jim Rohn

E liud Kipchoge, the legendary Kenyan marathon runner, is considered one of the greatest long-distance runners in history. He became the first person to run a marathon in under two hours, an achievement that seemed impossible for years. While Kipchoge's relentless discipline and work ethic were central to his success, one of the key factors that helped him achieve this incredible feat was the community he surrounded himself with.

Kipchoge trains in a small, rural village in Kenya with a group of other elite runners. Together, they live a modest lifestyle, sharing chores, eating simple meals, and motivating each other to push their limits. Every day, Kipchoge trains alongside his peers, many of whom are also world-class runners. This environment, rich in discipline and camaraderie, is designed to encourage peak performance.

Kipchoge has often credited his success not only to his personal effort but also to the group of runners who push him to be better each day. The mutual support, shared goals, and collective drive create an atmosphere where greatness thrives. Kipchoge's environment, both physical and social, is carefully crafted to promote success and foster good habits.

The lesson from Kipchoge's story is clear: surrounding yourself with people who share your values and goals can significantly impact your behavior and habits. Positive influence from others can accelerate your personal growth and make challenging goals feel more achievable.

Human beings are naturally social creatures. Whether we realize it or not, the people around us play a significant role in shaping our beliefs, attitudes, and behaviors. This influence extends to the habits we form. When we surround ourselves with people who prioritize healthy, productive habits, we are more likely to adopt those behaviors ourselves.

The reverse is also true. If we spend time with individuals who engage in unhealthy or unproductive behaviors, we risk being pulled in the same direction. This is why it is crucial to be intentional about the company we keep when striving to build new habits or break old ones.

Take a moment to evaluate the people you spend the most time with. Are they helping you move closer to your goals, or are they reinforcing bad habits? Habit builders are individuals who encourage your growth, support your positive habits, and challenge you to become better. They could be friends, family members, coworkers, or mentors.

Look for people who have already mastered the habits you want to adopt or who are on a similar journey of self-improvement. These individuals will inspire you to stay committed and will hold you accountable when your motivation wanes.

Accountability is one of the most powerful tools in habit formation. When you know that someone else is tracking your progress, you are more likely to stay consistent with your habits. Find a group of like-minded individuals who are working toward similar goals and establish a system of accountability. This could be a workout partner, a study group, or even an online community where members check in with each other regularly.

For example, if you are trying to build a habit of daily

exercise, find a friend who is committed to the same goal and set up regular workout sessions together. Knowing that someone else is counting on you to show up makes it harder to skip out on your commitment.

Mentorship can be a game-changer when it comes to building habits. A mentor is someone who has already walked the path you are on and can offer guidance, support, and encouragement. They can help you avoid common pitfalls, provide valuable insights, and hold you accountable to your goals.

If you are trying to develop a habit in a specific area—such as entrepreneurship, fitness, or personal development—seek out a mentor who has experience and success in that field. Their wisdom can save you time and effort, and their belief in your potential can motivate you to stay the course.

Just as it is important to surround yourself with habit builders, it is equally important to recognize and distance yourself from habit detractors. These are individuals who, whether intentionally or unintentionally, discourage your positive habits or encourage unhealthy behaviors. They may not share your goals or values, and their influence can make it harder for you to stay on track.

This doesn't mean cutting people out of your life completely, but it does mean setting boundaries. If certain friends always tempt you to skip your workouts or indulge in unhealthy eating, consider limiting your time with them, or choose activities that align with your goals when you do spend time together.

Peer pressure is often viewed in a negative light, but it can also be a powerful force for good. Positive peer pressure occurs when the people around you encourage and reinforce good habits. When everyone in your social circle is committed to growth and self-improvement, it creates a collective momentum that makes it easier for you to stay consistent.

For example, if you are trying to quit smoking, joining a support group of individuals who are also committed to quitting can provide the encouragement and accountability you need to succeed. Being part of a group where positive habits are the norm creates an environment where those habits become easier to maintain.

Your physical environment also plays a crucial role in shaping your habits. Just as the people around you influence your behavior, your surroundings can either make it easier or harder to stick to your habits. You can reduce friction and increase the likelihood of success by intentionally designing your environment to support your goals.

Take a look at your physical environment and ask yourself whether it is conducive to the habits you want to build. If you want to develop a habit of reading more, is there a comfortable reading nook in your home? If you are trying to eat healthier, is your kitchen stocked with nutritious foods, or is it filled with tempting junk food?

Small changes to your environment can have a big impact on your behavior. Rearrange your space to make good habits more accessible and bad habits less convenient. For example, if you want to practice mindfulness, create a designated meditation space in your home. If you are trying to cut down on screen time, keep your phone in another room while you work.

Visual cues can serve as powerful reminders to stay consistent with your habits. For example, if you are trying to build a habit of drinking more water, keep a water bottle on your desk where you can see it throughout the day. If you are working on a fitness habit, lay out your workout clothes the night before so that they're ready to go in the morning.

These small cues serve as constant reminders of your commitment and make it easier to follow through on your habits.

Habits are easier to maintain when they are embedded into a routine. Structure your day in a way that naturally incorporates the habits you are trying to build. For example, if you want to establish a habit of journaling, set aside a specific time each morning or evening to write in your journal. By attaching your habits to existing routines, they become automatic and require less conscious effort over time.

The people and environment around you have a profound impact on your ability to build and maintain habits. By intentionally surrounding yourself with habit builders—those who share your goals and encourage your growth—you can create a positive feedback loop that makes habit formation easier and more sustainable.

Remember, you have the power to shape both your social circle and your physical environment. Choose wisely, and you'll find that your journey toward habit mastery becomes smoother and more enjoyable. Surround yourself with people who lift you up, and design an environment that supports your success.

Law Thirteen

Link Effort with Satisfaction

"The greatest reward for doing is the opportunity to do more." — Jim Rohn

L inking effort with satisfaction is a fundamental aspect of habit formation. Our brains are wired to seek pleasure and avoid pain, making the experience of reward crucial for reinforcing behaviors. When we associate specific actions with positive feelings or rewards, we create a feedback loop that encourages us to repeat those behaviors.

The concept of reward in habit-building can be explained through the framework of operant conditioning, a psychological principle where behaviors are reinforced or diminished based on the consequences that follow. Positive reinforcement, such as rewards, increases the likelihood that a behavior will be repeated in the future. This is why it is essential to incorporate immediate rewards into the habit-building process.

To effectively link effort with satisfaction, start by identifying what rewards resonate with you. These can be simple pleasures or meaningful treats that motivate you. For example, if you are working on a fitness habit, consider rewarding yourself with a relaxing bubble bath, a movie night, or your favorite snack after completing a workout.

The key is to choose rewards that genuinely bring you joy and reinforce the positive behavior you are trying to cultivate. Be mindful of the type of reward you select; it should support your overall goals rather than undermine them.

Once you have identified your rewards, create a system to track your progress and celebrate your achievements. This could be as simple as maintaining a habit tracker or journal where you record your efforts and rewards. For every milestone or completed task, treat yourself to a reward.

For instance, if your goal is to read more books, reward yourself with a small treat for every book you finish or create a more significant reward for every five books. This structured approach creates clear connections between effort and satisfaction, making it easier to stay motivated.

It is crucial to recognize and celebrate small wins along the way, not just the big milestones. Each small accomplishment deserves acknowledgment. By focusing on progress rather than perfection, you cultivate a positive mindset that keeps you motivated.

For example, if you are working on improving your writing skills, celebrate completing a writing session, finishing a chapter, or submitting a piece of work. Treat yourself to something enjoyable, like a coffee date with a friend or a small shopping spree. These small celebrations create a sense of satisfaction that fuels your commitment to your habit.

One of the most effective ways to link effort with satisfaction is to ensure that rewards are immediate. The closer the reward is to the behavior you want to reinforce, the stronger the association will be.

For example, if you are trying to develop a habit of drinking more water, reward yourself with a refreshing beverage or snack immediately after drinking a certain amount of water. This creates a direct connection between the action and the reward, making it more likely that you will continue the habit.

Sharing your achievements and progress with friends or

family can amplify the sense of satisfaction associated with your efforts. When you talk about your accomplishments, you reinforce the positive feelings associated with your hard work.

Consider joining a community or support group related to your goals, where members celebrate each other's successes. The encouragement and positive reinforcement from others create an uplifting environment that fosters motivation and commitment.

Linking effort with satisfaction extends beyond individual habits; it can shape your entire approach to life. By adopting a habit-driven lifestyle that emphasizes enjoyment and fulfillment, you can create a positive feedback loop that leads to continuous growth and achievement.

Embrace a growth mindset that celebrates progress over perfection. Understand that setbacks and challenges are part of the journey, and focus on learning from each experience. This mindset shift allows you to find satisfaction in the effort you put forth rather than solely in the outcomes.

Take time to reflect on your journey and acknowledge how far you have come. Celebrating your progress can provide motivation and reinforce your commitment to the habits you are building. Keep a journal to document your efforts, challenges, and successes. This reflection allows you to appreciate the effort you have invested and the satisfaction that comes from each step forward.

Finally, strive to make your daily routine enjoyable. Seek ways to incorporate fun and pleasure into the activities you engage in, whether it is through music, social interactions, or enjoyable environments. When you find joy in the process, the effort feels less burdensome and more rewarding.

Linking effort with satisfaction is a powerful principle that can transform your habit-building journey. You pave the way for lasting success by recognizing and celebrating your achievements, creating rewarding experiences, and maintaining a positive mindset.

To illustrate this, here's a story about a small town, where there was an ice cream shop called "Sweet Success," owned by a passionate entrepreneur named Maria. She opened her shop with a dream of sharing her love for ice cream with the community. Maria was determined to make her business a success, but the early days were tough. She faced long hours, fluctuating sales, and the constant pressure of running a small business.

To keep herself motivated during those challenging times, Maria developed a habit of treating herself to a scoop of her favorite ice cream after completing a particularly difficult task or achieving a small milestone in her business. For example, after a long day of inventory management or when she finally secured a catering contract, she would reward herself with a scoop of caramel swirl ice cream. This simple yet effective strategy helped her connect her hard work with immediate gratification, reinforcing her commitment to her goals.

As her business grew, Maria realized that the key to her success lay not only in her dedication to her craft but also in the satisfaction she derived from each small victory. She learned that linking effort with enjoyment made the arduous journey of entrepreneurship much more fulfilling. Maria's ice cream shop flourished, and she eventually expanded her offerings to include creative flavors and unique toppings, turning "Sweet Success" into a beloved community staple.

Maria's story illustrates the importance of linking effort with satisfaction. By recognizing her accomplishments and treating herself to a reward, she maintained her motivation and commitment to her business. This principle applies to any goal or habit you want to cultivate in your own life.

Maria used simple rewards to sustain her motivation during challenging times. By consciously linking your actions to immediate rewards, you can create a fulfilling habit-driven lifestyle that makes the process enjoyable and satisfying. Ultimately, this connection between effort and satisfaction becomes the key to unlocking your potential and achieving your goals.

Law Fourteen

Design Systems, Not Just Goals

"You do not rise to the level of your goals. You fall to the level of your systems." — James Clear

S am was a talented musician with dreams of performing on grand stages. From a young age, he had aspirations of becoming a renowned guitarist, driven by the desire to play like his idols. Sam set ambitious goals for himself, such as mastering a particular song within a month or performing at local venues every few weeks. While these goals motivated him initially, he soon realized that without a structured approach, his progress was inconsistent.

One day, after a particularly disappointing practice session where he struggled with basic chords, Sam had an epiphany. He decided to shift his focus from lofty goals to creating a system that would support his daily practice. Instead of fixating on mastering specific songs within a set timeframe, he established a daily routine that included dedicated practice time, warm-ups, and a mix of technical exercises. He designed a schedule that allowed him to gradually improve his skills without the pressure of immediate results.

By focusing on the system rather than the outcome, Sam found that he became more consistent in his practice. He played every day, no matter how small the improvement, and celebrated the process rather than the product. Over time, his skills flourished. Sam's system of daily practice, combined with patience and persistence, led to the mastery of complex pieces and ultimately, the opportunity to perform at a major music festival.

Sam's story highlights the power of designing systems rather than just setting goals. While goals provide direction, it is the systems we create that sustain progress and lead to lasting success.

When it comes to building habits, systems are the backbone that supports your journey. Goals may set the destination, but systems outline the route you take to get there. Focusing on systems provides a framework that helps you maintain consistent action, regardless of immediate results or setbacks.

Goals are the specific outcomes you aim to achieve, such as losing weight, completing a project, or learning a new skill. While they are important for providing motivation and direction, they can sometimes lead to frustration when progress stalls. This is where systems come into play.

Systems, on the other hand, are the daily practices and processes that enable you to make progress toward your goals. They include the habits, routines, and workflows you establish to support your journey. When you have a well-designed system in place, you can focus on the actions you need to take daily, rather than becoming overwhelmed by the end result.

One of the most significant advantages of designing systems is sustainability. A well-crafted system allows you to build habits that endure over time, even in the face of challenges. When you rely solely on goals, the pressure to achieve can lead to burnout or disappointment. However, when you focus on systems, you create a flexible approach that accommodates the ups and downs of life.

For example, if your goal is to read 12 books in a year, you might feel discouraged if you miss a month. But if you have a system in place where you read for 30 minutes every day, you can maintain that habit regardless of the number of books you finish. The system becomes the priority, allowing you to enjoy the process without fixating on the end result.

Before you can design effective systems, start by defining your goals. What do you want to achieve? Be specific and realistic about your objectives. Once you have clarity on your goals, you can create systems that align with them.

To develop systems that support your goals, break them down into smaller, actionable steps. Identify the daily or weekly actions you need to take to move closer to your objectives. For instance, if your goal is to get fit, your actionable steps might include scheduling workout sessions, planning meals, and tracking your progress.

Design daily routines that incorporate the actions you identified. Consistency is key to building effective systems, so aim to integrate your habits into your life seamlessly. For example, if your goal is to write a book, establish a routine of writing for a set amount of time each day. This habit will help you build momentum over time, allowing your writing to flourish.

Keep track of your progress within your systems. Use journals, habit trackers, or digital tools to monitor your daily actions. Regularly review your progress to identify what's working and what may need adjustment. This reflection allows you to stay accountable and make necessary tweaks to your systems as you go along.

While it is essential to have systems in place, it is equally important to remain flexible. Life can throw unexpected challenges your way, and rigid systems can lead to frustration. Be willing to adapt your systems as needed while staying committed to your overall goals. Flexibility ensures that you continue moving forward, even if your path changes.

Shift your focus from the end result to the daily actions that lead you there. Celebrate your efforts and progress, no matter how small. Recognizing the importance of the journey will keep you motivated and engaged, making it easier to maintain your systems.

When you prioritize systems over goals, the benefits extend beyond the immediate outcomes. A well-designed system can create a ripple effect that influences various aspects of your life.

As you consistently follow your systems and see progress, your confidence grows. Each small victory reinforces your belief in your ability to achieve your goals. This confidence empowers you to take on more significant challenges and push beyond your comfort zone.

Focusing on systems fosters a mindset of continuous improvement. When you prioritize the process, you become more open to learning and adapting along the way. This lifelong learning mindset allows you to embrace challenges as opportunities for growth.

Creating systems that promote healthy habits contributes to your overall well-being. Whether it is through physical fitness, mental health practices, or productive routines, establishing sustainable systems can lead to a more balanced and fulfilling life.

In your journey toward achieving your goals, remember that the key lies in designing systems, not just setting goals. Like

Sam, the musician who shifted his focus to daily practice, you can create processes that make progress sustainable over time.

By breaking down your goals, establishing routines, and celebrating the journey, you empower yourself to create lasting change. Embrace the power of systems, and watch as they transform your habits, mindset, and overall life.

Once Again...

Design systems, not just goals.

Law Fifteen

Never Rely on Motivation

"You cannot rely on motivation. You have to rely on your system." — *James Clear*

Motivation can be a powerful catalyst for change, but it is inherently unpredictable. It can surge when we feel inspired and dwindle in times of stress or fatigue. This inconsistency can lead to frustration, especially when we find ourselves waiting for the "right" moment to take action.

Motivation is often viewed as the driving force behind our actions. However, relying solely on motivation can create a precarious foundation for habit-building. Life is filled with obstacles, distractions, and challenges that can drain our motivation. When we depend on fleeting feelings of inspiration to fuel our efforts, we risk falling into a cycle of inconsistency.

Motivation can be influenced by various factors, such as our environment, emotions, and even the people we surround ourselves with. It often feels like a wave—sometimes crashing over us with enthusiasm and other times receding, leaving us stranded. This volatility can make it difficult to establish habits that endure over time.

To cultivate lasting habits, it is essential to focus on creating systems that support your goals and actions. Systems provide a structure that allows you to take consistent action, regardless of your motivation level. Here's how systems can anchor your habits:

Systems provide a framework that organizes your daily activities and routines. By designing specific processes that dictate how you approach your goals, you create a pathway that keeps you moving forward, even when motivation wanes. For example, a student who sets aside dedicated study hours each week is more likely to stay on track with their learning, regardless of how motivated they feel at any given moment.

When habits are tied to a system, they become automatic. This automation reduces the need for willpower and decision-making, which can be mentally taxing. For instance, if you want to eat healthier, preparing meals in advance and having healthy snacks readily available removes the temptation to indulge in less nutritious options when motivation is low. Your system streamlines your choices, making it easier to stick to your goals.

Establishing systems can also enhance accountability. Sharing your goals with a friend or joining a community of like-minded individuals creates a support network that helps you stay on track. This accountability reinforces your commitment to the system and ensures that you remain focused on your actions, regardless of your motivation level. Jenna, for instance, found that joining a running group provided her with both encouragement and a sense of responsibility to show up.

To build a system, start by clarifying your goals and values. What do you want to achieve, and why is it important to you? Having a clear understanding of your motivations will guide you in creating systems that resonate with your aspirations.

Create daily routines that incorporate the actions needed to move toward your goals. Break down larger objectives into smaller, manageable tasks. This approach makes it easier to take consistent action and reduces overwhelm.

To overcome resistance, make it as easy as possible to start your desired habits. Remove barriers that may hinder your progress. For example, if your goal is to exercise regularly, lay out your workout clothes the night before or keep your gym bag packed and ready to go. The less friction there is, the more likely you are to take action.

Incorporate reminders and cues into your environment to trigger the desired behaviors. This could be setting alarms for your training sessions, placing sticky notes on your bathroom mirror, or using habit-tracking apps. These cues serve as gentle nudges that keep your goals at the forefront of your mind.

Use tracking tools to monitor your progress and celebrate your achievements. This practice reinforces the positive behaviors you are cultivating and helps you stay accountable to your systems. Over time, tracking creates a visual representation of your efforts, motivating you to continue.

Regularly review your systems to assess their effectiveness. Are they helping you make progress? If something is not working, do not be afraid to adjust your approach. Flexibility is essential for maintaining a sustainable system that supports your growth.

By building systems, you cultivate resilience and adaptability. When motivation fluctuates, your commitment to the process remains strong. You learn to navigate challenges and keep moving forward, fostering a growth mindset that embraces progress over perfection.

Systems help develop a habitual mindset that prioritizes consistent action. Over time, your habits become ingrained in your routine, making it easier to maintain momentum. This habitual mindset can extend beyond one area of your life, influencing your overall approach to challenges.

When you focus on systems rather than motivation, you set yourself up for long-term success. Sustainable habits built on strong systems lead to lasting change, helping you achieve your goals and aspirations over time.

Jenna is an aspiring athlete with dreams of competing in marathons. Like many, she was initially driven by bursts of motivation, especially when she signed up for her first race. The excitement of the upcoming event fueled her desire to train. Jenna started strong, waking up early to run and pushing herself during workouts. However, as the weeks progressed, that initial motivation began to wane.

When she faced challenging days or bad weather, her enthusiasm faded, and her training became sporadic. Jenna would skip her runs, convincing herself she would catch up later. As the race date approached, she realized she hadn't adequately prepared. In a moment of reflection, Jenna recognized that she had been relying on motivation to drive her actions rather than establishing a consistent routine.

Determined to turn things around, she decided to create a system that would support her training, regardless of how she felt. Jenna developed a training schedule that included specific running days, strength training, and recovery periods. She also joined a running group to stay accountable and inspired. As a result, even on days when she didn't feel like running, Jenna followed her plan, and her training became a part of her lifestyle.

On race day, Jenna crossed the finish line not only because she had shown up but because she had built a solid system that ensured her success. Her story serves as a powerful reminder that while motivation may spark our desires, it is our systems that carry us through the challenges we face.

While motivation can ignite your passion and drive, it is ultimately the systems you create that will carry you through the ebbs and flows of life. Just like Jenna, the athlete who learned to rely on her training system, you too can cultivate habits that withstand the test of time.

Embrace the power of systems in your habit-building journey. By focusing on structure, automation, accountability, and adaptability, you'll create a foundation that supports your growth and success, regardless of the motivation you may or may not feel at any given moment. Remember, it is not about waiting for the right motivation; it is about creating the right systems that will help you thrive.

Once Again...

Law Sixteen

Practice with Purpose

"Repetition is the mother of all learning." — A. R. Rahman

Anaya, from a young age was captivated by the melodious sounds of the violin. After years of dedication and practice, she finally landed a spot in one of the city's prestigious orchestras. On her first day, she was thrilled yet intimidated by the caliber of her fellow musicians. They were seasoned professionals, and Anaya felt the weight of their expectations. During the rehearsal, she played her part flawlessly, but something felt off. The conductor noticed it too. "Anaya," he said gently, "You're playing well, but are you practicing with purpose? Repetition without intention will not elevate your performance."

Anaya took these words to heart. That evening, instead of mindlessly running through her pieces, she focused on specific sections that needed improvement. She recorded herself, listened critically, and sought feedback from her mentor. With each deliberate practice session, she transformed her skills. Over time, her playing became not just a mechanical task but a soulful expression of her dedication. By practicing with purpose, she not only improved her technique but also developed a deeper connection to her music, ultimately earning her a solo performance at the orchestra's annual concert.

Anaya's story serves as a reminder that simply repeating a habit does not guarantee mastery. It requires intention and reflection to truly refine skills. This concept is applicable in various aspects of life, whether in sports, art, or even daily routines. Practicing with purpose transforms routine actions into deliberate steps toward mastery.

When we engage in any activity, be it exercising, studying, or working on a craft, the tendency is often to repeat the same actions without much thought. This mindless repetition can lead to stagnation. However, by focusing on specific aspects of the habit we wish to improve, we can enhance our overall performance. For example, a runner might continuously jog every morning but see little improvement in speed. However, if they focus on specific techniques, like their breathing or stride, their performance can drastically improve. This shift from mindless repetition to purposeful practice is where real growth occurs.

Deliberate practice involves setting clear goals for each session. Instead of saying, "I will practice the guitar today," one might say, "I will work on my finger placement and strumming technique for 30 minutes." This level of specificity allows for measurable progress and reinforces the habit. As you engage in purposeful practice, you will notice areas that need attention, which fosters a sense of ownership and control over your development.

Incorporating feedback into your practice routine is also essential. Mentors and peers can offer insights that you might overlook, allowing you to refine your approach further. Feedback creates a loop of improvement, encouraging you to adjust your techniques and strategies. This can be especially beneficial in team environments, where collaboration can lead to heightened creativity and innovative solutions.

Moreover, celebrating small victories along the way is crucial. Each step toward mastery, no matter how small, deserves recognition. This not only boosts your motivation but also reinforces the habit. By acknowledging progress, you connect the effort with satisfaction, creating a positive feedback loop that makes it easier to continue practicing with purpose.

Ultimately, mastering a habit requires more than just repetition; it necessitates a commitment to improvement. By engaging in deliberate practice, setting specific goals, seeking feedback, and celebrating progress, you can turn mere repetition into a powerful tool for growth. Remember, the journey to mastery is not a sprint; it is a marathon fueled by intention and dedication.

Once Again...

PRACTICE WITH PURPOSE

Law Seventeen

Use Cues to Trigger Action

"You will never change your life until you change something you do daily." — John C. Maxwell

David struggled with his health. Over the years, his busy lifestyle and poor eating habits led to weight gain and decreased energy. Despite knowing he needed to make changes, he often felt overwhelmed and unsure of where to start. One day, while sitting in a café, he overheard a conversation between two friends discussing their fitness journeys. They spoke about the importance of creating cues that prompted them to take action. Intrigued, David began to reflect on his own routines and what cues he could establish to trigger healthier habits.

Determined to make a change, David sat down and identified specific cues that could help him adopt healthier behaviors. He decided that every morning, right after brushing his teeth, he would place a water bottle on his kitchen counter. This simple act served as a visual reminder to hydrate and kickstart his day. Additionally, he placed his running shoes by the front door, making it easier to grab them on his way out for a morning jog. These intentional cues transformed his mornings. Instead of feeling sluggish and unmotivated, he found himself reaching for the water bottle and slipping on his shoes with newfound enthusiasm.

Cues serve as triggers that prompt specific actions, creating a clear path for desired behaviors. By strategically designing your environment and daily routines, you can foster the habits you wish to cultivate while diminishing those you want to diminish.

In habit formation, cues can take many forms. They can be visual reminders, auditory signals, or even emotional states. For instance, you might use a specific time of day as a cue, such as setting an alarm for 7 a.m. to signal the start of your morning workout. Alternatively, you might create an emotional cue by associating a particular song with a workout session. When you hear that song, it triggers the motivation to exercise. This association can significantly enhance your commitment to the habit over time.

The key to using cues effectively lies in consistency. By ensuring that your cues are consistent and reliable, you strengthen the connection between the trigger and the action. For example, if you consistently place your workout gear near your bed, you'll associate waking up with the action of getting ready to exercise. This association helps the habit take root in your daily routine, making it feel more automatic.

Another important aspect of cues is their ability to create

routines. When cues become a part of your regular schedule, they create a seamless flow that reinforces positive habits. Take Sarah for instance, a college student who struggled with procrastination. She recognized that her study habits often faltered when she felt overwhelmed by her workload. To counter this, she established a cue system. Every time she sat down at her desk to study, she lit a scented candle. The candle became a powerful cue that signaled her brain to focus and engage with her work. Over time, the mere act of lighting the candle became enough to trigger her study routine, allowing her to create a productive environment.

Moreover, cues can be personalized to suit your lifestyle and preferences. This customization can enhance your motivation to act. For example, if you enjoy reading but find it difficult to fit it into your day, you might place a book on your pillow each morning. This visual cue not only reminds you to read before bed but also creates a sense of anticipation. Personalizing cues to your interests and lifestyle fosters a deeper connection to the habit, increasing the likelihood of success.

However, it's essential to be mindful of negative cues that can hinder your progress. Just as positive cues can trigger desired behaviors, negative cues can lead to unwanted habits. For example, if you frequently find yourself mindlessly scrolling through social media when you see your phone on the table, it's crucial to address that cue. You might consider placing your phone in another room during work hours or using app-blocking software to reduce distractions. You create space for positive habits to thrive by removing negative cues from your environment.

Ultimately, the use of cues is a powerful tool for habit formation. By identifying and implementing strong triggers that prompt your desired actions, you can cultivate habits that align with your goals. Just as David transformed his mornings with simple visual reminders, you too can create cues that make your desired habits feel more accessible and automatic. Remember, the journey to mastering your habits begins with the intention to trigger action. Embrace the power of cues, and watch as your life gradually transforms, one habit at a time.

Once Again...

Use cues to trigger action.

Law Eighteen

Overhaul One Habit at a Time

"You can't improve what you don't measure." —
Peter Drucker

In the heart of New York City, there lived a young woman named Emily. Like many others, she found herself juggling numerous responsibilities; work, social commitments, and personal aspirations. Overwhelmed by the demands of life, she often felt stuck in a cycle of unhealthy habits. Whether it was her tendency to skip workouts, indulge in junk food, or procrastinate on important tasks, Emily knew that changes needed to be made. But every time she attempted to overhaul her lifestyle, she quickly became discouraged and gave up. It wasn't until she stumbled upon the concept of focusing on one habit at a time that her journey toward transformation truly began.

Determined to reclaim her life, Emily sat down with a notebook and made a list of the habits she wanted to change. Instead of trying to tackle them all at once, such as dieting, exercising regularly, and enhancing her productivity, she decided to concentrate on just one habit: exercise. Emily recognized that by dedicating her energy to this single goal, she could cultivate a more profound commitment to it. She started small, committing to a 20-minute workout every morning, gradually building her endurance and confidence.

Over the course of a few weeks, Emily began to notice a shift in her mindset. As her physical health improved, she felt more energized and motivated to take on other aspects of her life. By focusing on one habit at a time, she was not only able to establish a consistent workout routine but also gain momentum for other positive changes. Once she felt comfortable with her exercise routine, she shifted her attention to her diet, opting for healthier food choices. Emily made meaningful progress toward her overall well-being by concentrating on one habit at a time.

Transformation requires dedicated energy and attention, and attempting to overhaul multiple habits simultaneously can lead to feelings of overwhelm and failure. When you prioritize one habit, you can develop a sense of mastery and competence that fuels your motivation to tackle additional changes.

Research supports the notion that focusing on one habit leads to better outcomes. A study conducted by the University of California, Los Angeles, found that individuals who concentrated on changing one behavior at a time were more successful in sustaining that change than those who tried to adopt multiple habits simultaneously. This approach not only fosters a sense of accomplishment but also strengthens the neural pathways in the brain associated with the habit, making it easier to maintain in the long run.

When you embark on the journey of habit transformation, consider the process of habit stacking. After successfully establishing one habit, you can seamlessly build upon that foundation by adding another. This technique, often referred to as "habit stacking," involves pairing a new habit with an existing one to create a natural flow in your routine. For instance, after Emily felt confident with her exercise regimen, she decided to incorporate a habit of drinking a glass of water each morning right after her workout. By leveraging her existing routine, she created a structure that facilitated the adoption of additional positive behaviors.

Moreover, focusing on one habit at a time allows for reflection and adjustment. When you concentrate on a single behavior, you can observe how it affects your life and make necessary changes. For example, as Emily continued her fitness journey, she realized that early morning workouts were not the best fit for her lifestyle. Instead of forcing herself to adhere to this schedule, she experimented with different workout times until she discovered that exercising during her lunch break worked better for her. This adaptability was made possible because she had dedicated her energy to that one habit, allowing her to learn and grow through the process.

It's important to acknowledge that habit change is not always a linear process. There will be challenges and setbacks along the way. However, when you focus on one habit at a time, you develop resilience and the ability to bounce back from obstacles. Another advantage of focusing on one habit is that it creates a clearer sense of purpose. When you have a specific goal in mind, it becomes easier to measure your progress and celebrate your successes. Each small win reinforces your commitment and motivation.

Ultimately, the journey to transformation is best approached with a mindset of focus and dedication. By committing to overhaul one habit at a time, you create a foundation for lasting change. As you navigate this process, remember to be patient with yourself. Habit formation takes time, and the path may not always be straightforward. However, by concentrating your efforts and energy on one habit, you empower yourself to create meaningful and sustainable changes in your life.

Choose one habit that resonates with you and commit to it wholeheartedly. Embrace the process, learn from the challenges, and celebrate your successes along the way. In doing so, you'll discover the transformative power of focused habit change; one step at a time.

Once Again…

OVERHAUL
ONE HABIT
AT A TIME.

Law Nineteen

Make Your Habits Public

"Accountability is the glue that ties commitment to the result." — Bob Proctor

J ake had always dreamt of becoming a novelist. For years, he had jotted down ideas, created characters, and even outlined plots in the solitude of his room. However, when it came to actually writing his novel, Jake found himself consistently procrastinating. He was haunted by self-doubt, and without anyone to hold him accountable, his dream remained just that—a dream. One day, he decided to share his aspirations with a group of friends who regularly gathered for coffee and conversation.

At first, Jake felt vulnerable exposing his ambitions to others. He knew that revealing his goal would mean he would be expected to make progress and follow through. However, as he shared his story with his friends, something remarkable happened. They were not only supportive, but they also expressed genuine interest in his writing journey. They began asking him about his progress, checking in regularly, and even offering encouragement when he faced obstacles. This external pressure transformed the way Jake approached his goal.

Having made his aspirations public, Jake felt a newfound sense of accountability. The fear of disappointing his friends motivated him to put pen to paper. Each week, he committed to writing a certain number of words and would report back to the group during their coffee meetings. The mere act of sharing his goal and progress made it feel more real, shifting it from an abstract dream into a tangible pursuit. As he continued to write and receive encouragement, he gained confidence in his abilities, and his novel began to take shape.

When you share your goals and aspirations with others, you invite external motivation into your journey. This accountability can take many forms, whether it is sharing your goals with friends, joining a support group, or posting updates on social media. The desire to uphold commitments and avoid disappointing others can be a powerful force driving you to stay consistent in your habits.

Research supports the idea that public accountability enhances commitment and improves performance. A study published in the journal "Psychological Science" found that individuals who made their goals public were more likely to achieve them than those who kept their intentions private. The presence of external accountability fosters a sense of obligation, making individuals more likely to follow through on their commitments.

When making your habits public, it's essential to choose the right audience. Surround yourself with supportive and encouraging individuals who genuinely want to see you succeed. This might be friends, family members, colleagues, or even online communities with shared interests. Creating a positive and uplifting environment for your journey will help reinforce your commitment and propel you toward your goals.

Additionally, consider using social media as a platform for accountability. Sharing your goals, progress, and even challenges with a wider audience can foster a sense of community. You might be surprised by the number of people who resonate with your journey and offer their support. Social media can serve as a powerful tool for motivation, allowing you to connect with others who share similar aspirations and experiences.

In Jake's case, the public nature of his goal not only helped him stay on track but also opened up opportunities for collaboration and feedback. His friends, intrigued by his writing, began sharing their insights and suggestions, enhancing his creative process. By making his aspirations known, Jake cultivated a sense of shared ownership of his journey, transforming what once felt like a solitary pursuit into a collective effort.

While public accountability can be a strong motivator, it's

important to approach it with authenticity. Being open about your struggles and setbacks can foster deeper connections with others. Vulnerability allows you to create a supportive network that understands the ups and downs of habit formation. When you share not just your successes but also your challenges, you invite empathy and encouragement, reinforcing the bond between you and your accountability partners.

It's also vital to celebrate your milestones with your supporters. As you make progress toward your goals, share your achievements, no matter how small. Celebrating victories, whether it's finishing a chapter of your novel or sticking to a workout routine for a month, reinforces your commitment and encourages those around you to celebrate their own successes. This positive reinforcement creates a cycle of accountability and motivation, propelling everyone involved toward their goals.

However, be mindful of the potential pitfalls of public accountability. While external pressure can be motivating, it can also lead to feelings of anxiety or comparison if not approached carefully. Ensure that your accountability network is a source of positivity rather than competition. Focus on personal growth and celebrate individual journeys, fostering an environment where everyone feels valued and supported.

In conclusion, making your habits public can be a game-changer in your journey toward mastery. By inviting external accountability into your life, you create a powerful motivator to stay consistent and committed to your goals. Jake's experience serves as a reminder that sharing your aspirations not only holds you accountable but also cultivates a supportive community that enhances your growth. So, consider sharing your habits and goals with others: whether it's friends, family, or a wider audience. Embrace the power of public accountability and watch as it transforms your journey toward success.

Once Again…

Law Twenty

Build Habits for the Long Game

"Success is the sum of small efforts, repeated day in and day out." — *Robert Collier*

James Clear, a well-known author and habit expert, provides an excellent real-life example of building habits for the long game. Before becoming a prominent figure in the field of habit formation, Clear was an average student struggling with weight and fitness. In his early 20s, he found himself overweight and out of shape, feeling discouraged by the quick-fix solutions that promised instant results but ultimately failed him.

Instead of opting for another fad diet or an intensive workout program, Clear decided to adopt a more sustainable approach. He focused on making small, incremental changes to his lifestyle. He began with simple habits, such as walking daily and gradually increasing the intensity of his workouts. He incorporated healthy eating habits slowly, starting by eliminating one unhealthy food item at a time.

Clear's method was to focus on consistency rather than immediate results. His small, manageable changes eventually accumulated into significant improvements in his health and fitness. Over time, these habits became ingrained in his daily routine. The gradual approach not only helped him lose weight but also led him to write a bestselling book, "Atomic Habits", sharing his insights on building sustainable habits.

James Clear's story highlights the importance of focusing on long-term habits rather than quick fixes. His success came from consistent, small efforts that compounded over time, proving that sustainable change is built on incremental improvements rather than drastic measures.

Building habits for the long game requires a focus on sustainability and incremental progress. Instead of seeking immediate results, adopt small, manageable changes that fit into your daily routine. This approach helps create lasting habits that can be maintained over the long term.

Start by making gradual adjustments to your current routine.

For example, if your goal is to improve your health, begin with minor changes such as adding a short walk to your day or incorporating one healthy meal per week. As these habits become established, gradually increase their intensity and frequency.

Set realistic, long-term goals and celebrate small milestones along the way. Tracking your progress can provide motivation and reinforce your commitment. Remember, the key is consistency and patience. Over time, these small efforts will accumulate and lead to significant, sustainable results.

Law Twenty-one

Make Temptation Expensive

"Discipline is the bridge between goals and accomplishment." — *Jim Rohn*

Making temptation expensive involves creating obstacles that make undesirable behaviors less appealing. This can be achieved by increasing the effort, cost, or inconvenience associated with the bad habit.

For instance, if you are trying to curb impulsive spending, set up automatic transfers to a savings account and impose a waiting period before making non-essential purchases. By making it harder to engage in impulsive behavior, you can reduce its frequency and impact.

Additionally, consider the use of financial or social consequences to reinforce your commitment. Establish a system where you incur a penalty for engaging in unwanted behavior or seek support from friends or family to hold you accountable.

David Bach, a financial expert and author of "The Automatic Millionaire", faced a significant challenge with managing his spending habits. Early in his career, Bach struggled with overspending and mounting credit card debt. Recognizing the detrimental impact this had on his financial stability, he took decisive steps to make his spending habits more costly and less appealing.

Bach's strategy involved creating psychological and financial barriers to his impulsive spending. He set up an automatic savings plan where a portion of his income was directly deposited into a savings account before he even received his paycheck. This method made it more difficult for him to spend money impulsively, as it was out of sight and out of mind.

Additionally, Bach implemented a "spending freeze" strategy, where he imposed a waiting period before making non-essential purchases. He would wait 24 hours before deciding whether to buy something, allowing him to evaluate if the purchase was truly necessary or if it was driven by impulse.

The result of these strategies was a significant improvement in Bach's financial health. By making it more difficult and costly to engage in impulsive spending, he was able to focus on saving and investing, ultimately leading to financial stability and success. His story demonstrates how creating barriers to temptation can lead to better financial discipline and overall well-being.

Creating a supportive environment for positive habits is equally important. Make it easy to engage in desired behaviors by removing barriers and providing incentives. By designing your environment to support your goals, you enhance your ability to maintain positive habits and reduce the appeal of negative ones.

Once Again…

MAKE TEMPTATION EXPENSIVE.

Law Twenty-two

Associate Pain with the Old, Pleasure with the New

"People do not change because they see the light; they change because they feel the heat." — Andy Stanley

ssociating pain with old habits and pleasure with new ones is a powerful strategy for changing behavior. You can shift your behavior more effectively by creating a strong emotional link between negative outcomes and undesirable habits, and positive experiences and new habits.

Start by identifying the negative aspects of your old habit. Document how the behavior impacts your life negatively and use this information to create a strong association with discomfort. This helps to make the old habit less appealing.

Simultaneously, focus on the benefits and pleasures of your new habits. Engage in activities that you find enjoyable and rewarding. By creating positive associations with your new behaviors, you increase their attractiveness and reinforce your commitment to change.

Visualization can also play a crucial role. Imagine the positive outcomes of your new habits and how they contribute to your overall well-being. This mental exercise makes the new habits feel more achievable and motivating.

Tom Corley, author of "Rich Habits: The Daily Success Habits of Wealthy Individuals", provides an illustrative example of how associating pain with old habits and pleasure with new ones can drive significant change. Corley was once in a difficult financial situation, struggling with debt and poor financial habits. He realized that his lifestyle was unsustainable and needed to change.

Corley began by tracking his daily activities and expenditures, identifying how his current habits were contributing to his financial problems. He associated the discomfort of his debt and financial stress with his old habits, which motivated him to make a change.

To shift his focus, Corley adopted new, positive financial habits. He created a budget, started saving and investing regularly, and focused on improving his financial literacy. These new habits provided immediate satisfaction and a sense of accomplishment. He began to associate the positive outcomes of his new habits, such as financial security and personal growth, with pleasure.

As Corley continued to implement these changes, he found that the positive reinforcement of his new habits outweighed the discomfort of his old ones. His financial situation improved significantly, and he was able to build wealth and achieve his long-term financial goals. His story demonstrates the power of associating pain with negative behaviors and pleasure with positive changes to drive lasting transformation.

By consciously linking old habits with pain and new habits with pleasure, you can effectively drive behavior change and build lasting, positive habits.

Law Twenty-three

Master Your Mornings

"The way you start your day determines how well you live your day." — *Robin Sharma*

Mastering your mornings involves creating a structured routine that sets a positive tone for the rest of your day. The first few hours of the day have a significant impact on your productivity and overall well-being. You can enhance your focus and performance throughout the day by establishing a consistent morning routine.

Start by identifying activities that help you feel energized and focused. This could include exercise, meditation, journaling, or planning your day. Incorporate these activities into your morning routine to create a sense of purpose and direction.

Consistency is key. Stick to your morning routine even on weekends or days off to build a strong habit. Over time, these morning rituals will become ingrained in your daily routine, providing a solid foundation for success.

Track your progress and make adjustments as needed. If you find that certain activities are not as effective as others, experiment with different routines until you find what works best for you. By mastering your mornings, you can set yourself up for a productive and fulfilling day.

Tim Ferriss is an author who is renowned for his productivity strategies and time management techniques. In his quest to optimize his life, Ferriss discovered that the key to high performance and productivity lay in mastering his mornings.

Ferriss adopted a morning routine that he referred to as "The 4-Hour Workweek Morning Routine." His day began with a set of deliberate activities designed to set a productive tone for the rest of the day. This routine included exercise, meditation, and a review of his goals and priorities. By focusing on these activities first thing in the morning, Ferriss created a strong foundation for a successful day.

The impact of his morning routine was profound. Ferriss found that starting his day with intention and focus significantly enhanced his productivity and overall well-being. His morning habits not only boosted his performance at work but also contributed to a balanced and fulfilling personal life.

Ferriss's story illustrates the power of a well-structured morning routine. By establishing productive habits early in the day, you can create momentum and set yourself up for success. Mastering your mornings can lead to improved productivity, better focus, and a more fulfilling life.

Law Twenty-four

Use Time to Compound Your Results

"Success is not a destination, but the road that you are on." — Marlon Wayans

Using time to compound your results involves leveraging the power of consistency and long-term effort. Small, positive actions taken regularly can lead to substantial results over time. This principle applies to various areas of life, including investments, personal growth, and habit formation.

Start by setting clear, long-term goals and focusing on incremental progress. For example, if you are saving for retirement, consistently contribute to your savings or investment accounts. The compounding effect will lead to significant growth over time.

Patience is crucial. The benefits of compounding are not always immediately apparent, but consistent effort will pay off in the long run. Track your progress and make adjustments as needed, but avoid getting discouraged by short-term setbacks.

By understanding and harnessing the power of compounding,

you can achieve remarkable results and build a solid foundation for future success. Focus on making steady progress and trust in the process of compounding over time.

Warren Buffett, the legendary investor and chairman of Berkshire Hathaway, is a prime example of how the power of compounding can lead to extraordinary success. Buffett's investment strategy emphasizes the importance of long-term thinking and the compounding effect of time.

Buffett's investment philosophy revolves around the principle of buying quality stocks and holding them for the long term. He famously says, "Our favorite holding period is forever." This approach allows him to benefit from the compounding growth of his investments over many years.

One of Buffett's notable investments was his purchase of See's Candies in 1972. He paid $25 million for the company, which was considered a substantial investment at the time. Over the decades, See's Candies generated substantial profits, and Buffett's investment grew significantly in value. The compounding effect of long-term investment allowed Buffett to achieve remarkable returns on his initial investment.

Buffett's success story demonstrates the power of compounding over time. By focusing on long-term growth and allowing your investments or efforts to accumulate, you can achieve significant results. The key is to remain patient and consistent, trusting in the compounding effect of time.

Once Again...

Use time to compound your results.

Law Twenty-five

Make Habits Unavoidable

"Design your life so that it is impossible to fail." — *Naval Ravikant*

BJ Fogg, a behavior scientist, has extensively studied how to design environments that promote behavior change. His personal and professional experiences illustrate the effectiveness of making habits unavoidable by designing supportive environments.

Fogg's approach to behavior change involves creating an

environment where the desired behavior is the path of least resistance. For example, he wanted to establish a habit of flossing his teeth daily. To make the habit unavoidable, he placed the floss next to his toothbrush. This simple adjustment ensured that flossing was a natural extension of his existing brushing routine.

In his research, Fogg has applied this principle to help others build habits. He encourages people to design their environments to make positive behaviors easier to perform and negative behaviors more difficult. By removing barriers and creating cues for desired behaviors, you increase the likelihood of success.

Fogg's personal and professional successes in habit formation demonstrate the power of environmental design. By making habits unavoidable through thoughtful design, you can create a supportive environment that fosters positive behaviors and reduces the effort required to maintain them.

Making habits unavoidable involves designing your environment to support the desired behavior and minimize obstacles. You increase the likelihood of success by creating an environment where performing the habit is the path of least resistance.

Start by identifying the habit you want to establish and consider how you can make it easier to perform. For example, if you want to drink more water, keep a water bottle on your desk or carry one with you throughout the day. This simple change ensures that drinking water becomes a regular part of your routine.

Conversely, make it harder to engage in undesirable behaviors by increasing the effort or inconvenience associated with them. If you are trying to cut down on social media usage, remove apps from your phone or use website blockers to limit access.

Design your environment to provide cues and reminders for your desired habits. Place visual reminders or set up triggers that prompt you to engage in the behavior. By making habits unavoidable, you create a supportive environment that encourages positive behaviors and reduces the effort required to maintain them.

Habit Mastery Begins in the Mind

"Whether you think you can, or you think you can't; you are right." — *Henry Ford*

Habit mastery begins in the mind. Visualizing your desired habits and outcomes can enhance your ability to execute them successfully. Mental rehearsal prepares your mind for action, making it easier to perform the habit when the time comes.

Start by setting aside time each day for visualization. Imagine yourself successfully performing the habit, experiencing the associated sensations and emotions. This mental practice helps build confidence and reinforces your commitment to the habit.

Incorporate specific details into your visualization, such as the environment, the actions involved, and the desired outcome. This level of detail helps create a vivid mental image and prepares you for real-life execution.

Michael Phelps, the most decorated Olympian of all time, is renowned not just for his physical prowess but for his mental preparation. His success in swimming can be attributed significantly to his use of mental rehearsal—a practice that demonstrates how habit mastery begins in the mind.

Before every competition, Phelps engaged in detailed visualization exercises. He would mentally rehearse every stroke, turn, and finish of his races. This mental practice helped him anticipate and prepare for various scenarios, reducing anxiety and enhancing his performance. He described visualizing the race as if he were already swimming, experiencing every sensation and movement in his mind.

Phelps' mental rehearsal became a critical component of his training regimen. By envisioning his success and mentally preparing for different race situations, he was able to solidify his physical habits and build a winning mindset. This mental preparation not only improved his performance but also contributed to his remarkable consistency and focus.

Phelps' story illustrates the importance of mental rehearsal in mastering habits. By visualizing success and mentally preparing for challenges, you can strengthen your commitment and increase your likelihood of achieving your goals.

Mental rehearsal also aids in overcoming obstacles and setbacks. By envisioning potential challenges and planning how to address them, you can strengthen your resolve and increase your chances of success. Remember, habit mastery starts with a strong mental foundation.

Once Again…

HABIT MASTERY
BEGINS IN THE MIND.

Law Twenty-seven

Use Pain as a Teacher

"Failure is simply the opportunity to begin again, this time more intelligently." — *Henry Ford*

J.K. Rowling, the author of the Harry Potter series, experienced significant setbacks and failures before achieving unprecedented success. Her journey is a powerful example of how pain and failure can be used as teachers.

Before Rowling became a household name, she faced numerous rejections from publishers. At one point, she was a struggling single mother living on welfare, with her manuscript rejected by multiple publishers. The pain of these rejections was a significant setback, but Rowling used it as an opportunity to refine her work and persist.

Instead of giving up, Rowling learned from her failures. She continued to revise her manuscript and remained committed to her vision. Her persistence paid off when Bloomsbury, a small publisher, took a chance on her book. The Harry Potter series eventually became a global phenomenon, transforming Rowling's life and establishing her as one of the most successful authors of all time.

Rowling's story demonstrates how pain and failure can provide valuable lessons. By reflecting on setbacks and using them to improve and adapt, you can build resilience and increase your chances of future success.

Using pain as a teacher involves analyzing setbacks and failures to gain valuable insights and improve your approach. Instead of viewing pain as a roadblock, consider it a learning opportunity that can guide you toward better strategies and solutions.

When faced with failure, take time to reflect on what went wrong. Identify the factors that contributed to the setback and consider how you can address them moving forward. This process helps you adapt and refine your approach, increasing your chances of success in future attempts.

Embrace resilience and persistence. Understand that setbacks are a natural part of the journey and can provide important feedback. Use the lessons learned from pain to enhance your skills, strategies, and overall approach to achieving your goals.

By viewing pain as a teacher and using it to inform your actions, you can turn setbacks into stepping stones for success.

Once Again…

- USE PAIN -
AS A TEACHER-

Law Twenty-eight

Integrate Habits with Your Identity

"Your identity is the single most important factor in the success of your habit formation." — James Clear

Integrating habits with your identity involves aligning your behaviors with the person you want to become. When your habits are tied to your self-image, they become more automatic and sustainable.

Start by defining the identity you want to adopt. For example, if you want to become a healthier person, view yourself as someone who prioritizes health and well-being. This shift in identity helps reinforce your commitment to adopting healthy habits.

Incorporate habits that reflect this new identity into your daily routine. If you see yourself as a fit and active person, make regular exercise and healthy eating a part of your lifestyle. Over time, these habits will become ingrained in your self-concept and feel like a natural extension of who you are.

Regularly reflect on your progress and reaffirm your new identity. Celebrate achievements that align with your new self-image and make adjustments as needed to stay on track. By integrating habits with your identity, you build a strong foundation for lasting success and personal growth.

Dwayne Johnson, known as "The Rock," is a prime example of how integrating habits with your identity can lead to remarkable success. Before becoming a global superstar and successful entrepreneur, Johnson was a professional wrestler who transformed his life through a powerful shift in identity.

Early in his career, Johnson faced significant challenges and was struggling to find his path. However, he embraced the identity of a relentless and disciplined individual. He began to integrate this identity into his daily habits, including a rigorous fitness routine and a strong work ethic. His commitment to this new identity drove him to excel both in wrestling and in his subsequent acting career.

Johnson's transformation involved more than just adopting new habits; it required a complete change in how he viewed himself. By embracing the identity of someone who is hardworking, disciplined, and successful, he was able to make these traits an integral part of his daily life. This shift in identity played a crucial role in his success and allowed him to achieve his goals.

Johnson's story demonstrates the power of aligning your habits with your identity. By integrating positive behaviors into your self-concept, you create a strong foundation for lasting change and success.

Once Again...

INTEGRATE HABITS WITH YOUR IDENTITY

Law Twenty-nine

Build Your Habits on Small Wins

"Success is the sum of small efforts, repeated day in and day out." — *Robert Collier*

Sara Blakely, the founder of Spanx, turned a simple idea into a billion-dollar business. Her journey from a struggling salesperson to a self-made billionaire exemplifies the power of building habits on small wins.

Blakely's entrepreneurial journey began with a modest goal: to create a better undergarment. Initially, her efforts were small and incremental. She spent years experimenting with prototypes and pitching her idea to potential investors. Her first major breakthrough came when she managed to get her product into a high-end department store. This was a small win, but it set the stage for future successes.

Instead of aiming for immediate, massive success, Blakely focused on achieving incremental milestones. Each small win, whether it was securing a new retail partner or receiving positive customer feedback, fueled her progress. She celebrated these victories and used them as motivation to tackle the next challenge.

Blakely's story shows that focusing on small wins can lead to significant achievements. By building on each success and maintaining a positive mindset, she turned a small idea into a global brand. Her approach underscores the importance of recognizing and leveraging small victories in the pursuit of larger goals.

Building your habits on small wins involves starting with manageable, achievable goals and gradually expanding them. Small victories create momentum and boost your confidence, making it easier to tackle larger challenges.

Begin by setting realistic and specific goals that you can achieve in the short term. For instance, if your aim is to improve your fitness, start with a goal of exercising for just 10 minutes a day. Once this becomes a habit, gradually increase the duration and intensity of your workouts.

Celebrate each small win along the way. Acknowledge your progress and reward yourself for reaching milestones. This positive reinforcement helps to build confidence and sustain motivation.

As you achieve small wins, use them as a foundation for further growth. Each success reinforces your commitment and prepares you for more significant challenges. By focusing on incremental progress, you create a pathway to long-term success.

Once Again...

BUILD YOUR HABITS
ON SMALL WINS

Law Thirty

Never Neglect the Foundation

"The best time to plant a tree was 20 years ago. The second-best time is now." — Chinese Proverb

Steve Jobs, co-founder of Apple Inc., is known for his revolutionary impact on technology and design. However, his success was built on a solid foundation established early in his career. Jobs' early experiences and his commitment to foundational principles played a crucial role in his later achievements.

Before launching Apple, Jobs worked with Steve Wozniak on

the early personal computers, and their partnership was grounded in a shared vision of innovation and quality. This foundation of technical excellence and a commitment to user experience became the bedrock of Apple's success.

When Jobs returned to Apple in 1997 after being ousted, he focused on revisiting and reinforcing the company's core values. He streamlined the product line, emphasizing simplicity and design excellence. By returning to the foundational principles that originally made Apple successful, Jobs was able to revive the company and drive it to new heights.

Jobs' story illustrates the importance of never neglecting the foundation. You create a strong base for achieving future success by reinforcing the core values and principles that underpin your efforts. A solid foundation enables you to build on past achievements and adapt to new challenges.

Never neglect the foundation when building habits or pursuing goals. A strong foundation consists of core principles and practices that support your long-term success. Revisiting and reinforcing these fundamentals is essential for sustained achievement.

Start by identifying the core principles that are central to your goals. For example, if you are working on personal development, focus on foundational practices such as self-discipline, time management, and continuous learning.

Regularly review and strengthen these foundational elements. Ensure that they remain integral to your daily routine and decision-making process. By maintaining a solid foundation, you create a resilient structure that supports your growth and helps you navigate challenges.

Revisit and refine your foundational practices as needed. Adapt them to changing circumstances and new goals while staying true to the core values that underpin your success. A strong foundation provides stability and direction, allowing you to build on your achievements and reach new heights.

Law Thirty-one

Celebrate Every Milestone

"Success is not the key to happiness. Happiness is the key to success. If you love what you are doing, you will be successful." — Albert Schweitzer

Celebrating every milestone is a crucial aspect of building and maintaining motivation. Recognizing and rewarding your achievements reinforces positive behavior and helps sustain momentum toward your long-term goals.

Start by setting clear milestones and celebrating each one as you achieve it. Whether it is completing a project, reaching a fitness goal, or making progress in a personal endeavor, take time to acknowledge and celebrate your success.

Choose meaningful ways to celebrate that resonate with you. This could include treating yourself to something special, sharing your success with friends and family, or reflecting on your accomplishments. Celebrations provide a sense of achievement and reinforce your commitment to your goals.

Regularly review your progress and celebrate not only the major milestones but also the smaller victories along the way. Each celebration helps to build positive associations with your goals and motivates you to continue striving for success. By celebrating every milestone, you create a positive and rewarding journey toward achieving your long-term objectives.

Oprah Winfrey's rise from a challenging childhood to becoming one of the most influential media moguls is a testament to the power of celebrating milestones. Winfrey's journey is marked by her ability to acknowledge and celebrate each achievement, no matter how small.

Early in her career, Oprah faced numerous obstacles, including a tumultuous upbringing and initial setbacks in the media industry. Despite these challenges, she focused on celebrating each milestone. When she launched The Oprah Winfrey Show, she celebrated the show's first successful season and used the momentum to drive further success.

Throughout her career, Oprah consistently celebrated her achievements and milestones. Whether it was her first Emmy win or the launch of her own network, she took time to recognize and celebrate each success. This practice not only reinforced her motivation but also inspired those around her.

Oprah's story highlights the importance of celebrating milestones in achieving long-term success. By acknowledging and celebrating your achievements, you maintain motivation and foster a positive mindset. Celebrations provide a sense of accomplishment and help you stay focused on your goals.

Law Thirty-Two

Know When to Pivot

"Change is the only constant in life." — Heraclitus

Instagram's journey from a simple photo-sharing app to a global social media giant is a prime example of knowing when to pivot. The story of Instagram's evolution highlights the importance of adaptability and strategic change.

Instagram was originally launched in 2010 under the name Burbn. The app was designed as a check-in tool with various features, including photo-sharing. However, the founders, Kevin Systrom and Mike Krieger, noticed that users were primarily interested in the photo-sharing aspect, while other features were underutilized.

Recognizing the potential in this singular focus, the founders decided to pivot. They stripped down Burbn to its core feature—photo-sharing—and redesigned it as Instagram. This strategic pivot allowed them to concentrate on what users loved most and streamline the app's functionality.

The result was a massive success. Instagram quickly gained popularity, attracting millions of users and eventually being acquired by Facebook for $1 billion in 2012. The decision to pivot from a multi-featured app to a focused photo-sharing platform was a turning point that set the stage for Instagram's meteoric rise.

Instagram's story illustrates the power of knowing when to pivot. By recognizing the need for change and focusing on what truly resonated with users, the founders were able to transform a struggling app into a highly successful platform. Adaptability and strategic change can lead to significant success and new opportunities.

Knowing when to pivot involves recognizing when your current approach is not yielding the desired results and being willing to make strategic changes. Pivoting allows you to adapt to new circumstances, seize emerging opportunities, and realign your efforts with your goals.

Start by evaluating your current strategies and assessing their effectiveness. If you are not achieving the desired outcomes, consider whether a pivot could improve your results. This could involve changing your approach, focusing on different aspects of your goals, or exploring new opportunities.

Be open to feedback and data. Use insights from your experiences and observations to guide your decision-making process. If you notice patterns or trends indicating that a shift is needed, take proactive steps to implement changes.

A successful pivot involves careful planning and execution. Clearly define the new direction, set achievable goals, and communicate the changes to stakeholders if applicable. Embrace adaptability and flexibility as you navigate the transition and work toward your revised objectives.

Once Again...

KNOW WHEN TO PIVOT.

Law Thirty-three

Build Resilience in Your Habits

"It is not the strongest of the species that survive, nor the most intelligent, but the one most responsive to change." — Charles Darwin

K obe Bryant, one of the greatest basketball players of all time, exemplifies how building resilience into your habits can lead to extraordinary success. Bryant's career was marked by numerous challenges and setbacks, but his resilience and determination helped him overcome obstacles and achieve greatness.

One of the most notable challenges in Bryant's career was his recovery from a serious Achilles tendon injury in 2013. The injury threatened to end his career, but Bryant's resilience and commitment to his rehabilitation were unwavering. He adopted a rigorous training and recovery regimen, focusing on every aspect of his physical and mental recovery.

Bryant's resilience extended beyond his recovery. Throughout his career, he faced intense competition and criticism but remained focused on his goals. He continued to refine his skills, work tirelessly, and adapt to evolving challenges. His resilience was evident in his performance and his ability to bounce back from adversity.

Bryant's story demonstrates the importance of building resilience into your habits. By developing a mindset that embraces challenges and persists through difficulties, you can navigate setbacks and continue progressing toward your goals. Resilience enables you to adapt, recover, and thrive despite obstacles.

Building resilience into your habits involves developing the mental and emotional strength to withstand challenges and setbacks. Resilient habits help you maintain focus, adapt to change, and persevere in the face of adversity.

Start by identifying potential challenges and obstacles that you may encounter in pursuit of your goals. Develop strategies to address these challenges and incorporate them into your routine. This could include building flexibility into your habits, setting contingency plans, and practicing stress management techniques.

Cultivate a positive mindset that embraces setbacks as opportunities for growth. View challenges as chances to learn and improve rather than as insurmountable barriers. Use setbacks as feedback to refine your approach and strengthen your resilience.

Regularly reflect on your progress and celebrate your

successes. Acknowledge the effort and persistence required to overcome obstacles, and use these reflections to reinforce your commitment to your goals. By building resilience into your habits, you create a strong foundation for navigating challenges and achieving long-term success.

Once Again…

Law Thirty-four

Create Habits Around Your Energy Levels

"Do not watch the clock; do what it does. Keep going." — Sam Levenson

Creating habits around your energy levels involves tailoring your activities to match your natural rhythms and energy fluctuations. You can enhance your productivity and overall effectiveness by aligning your habits with your peak energy times.

Start by identifying your energy patterns throughout the day. Determine when you feel most alert and focused, as well as when you experience energy dips. Use this information to schedule your most important and challenging tasks during your peak energy periods.

Incorporate activities that boost your energy levels into your routine. Regular exercise, healthy eating, and adequate rest contribute to maintaining optimal energy levels. Make time for these practices to support your overall well-being and enhance your performance.

Be flexible and adaptable. Your energy levels may vary from day to day, so adjust your schedule and habits as needed. Listen to your body and make changes to accommodate fluctuations in energy. By creating habits that align with your natural rhythms, you can optimize your productivity and achieve your goals more effectively.

Barack Obama, the 44th President of the United States, is known for his disciplined approach to managing his time and energy. His ability to create habits around his energy levels played a crucial role in his effectiveness and productivity.

Obama's daily routine was designed to align with his natural energy levels. He structured his workday to tackle high-priority tasks during his peak energy periods and reserved less demanding activities for when his energy was lower. For instance, he made important decisions and addressed complex issues in the morning when he was most alert. In the afternoons, he focused on meetings and less critical tasks.

Obama also emphasized the importance of regular exercise as part of his routine. He incorporated physical activity into his schedule to boost his energy levels and maintain his overall well-being. This practice not only helped him manage stress but also enhanced his productivity and focus.

By aligning his habits with his natural energy patterns, Obama was able to maximize his effectiveness and maintain a high level of performance throughout his presidency. His approach underscores the importance of creating habits that align with your energy levels to optimize productivity and achieve your goals.

Once Again...

CREATE HABITS
AROUND YOUR ENERGY LEVELS.

Law Thirty-five

Never Underestimate the Power of Compound Growth

"Compound interest is the eighth wonder of the world. He who understands it, earns it; he who doesn't, pays it." — Albert Einstein

C ompound growth is one of the most powerful forces in personal development and financial success. It revolves around the idea that small, consistent actions, when compounded over time, lead to exponential results. Whether you're improving your habits, building wealth, or advancing in your career, the secret lies in steady, incremental progress that multiplies with time.

Imagine a tiny snowball at the top of a hill. As it rolls down, it gathers more snow, growing larger and larger. By the time it reaches the bottom, it's massive, far beyond its original size. This is how compound growth works—what starts small can build into something enormous if given enough time and consistency.

The key to harnessing compound growth is to focus on making small, positive changes in your daily routines. Maybe you start by saving just a small portion of your income each month, or you dedicate ten minutes a day to learning a new skill. Perhaps you commit to daily exercise, even if it's only for a short time. These small efforts, when done consistently, compound into significant results over the long term.

But there's a catch—compound growth requires patience. At first, the results may seem insignificant, almost invisible. You might wonder if your efforts are even making a difference. But just like a snowball gains momentum, your small actions, repeated over time, will begin to snowball into something far more substantial.

I used to know a guy called Sam. Sam was a struggling entrepreneur. When Sam first started his business, he was drowning in debt and working long hours without seeing much progress. Frustrated but determined, he decided to focus on just one thing—improving his customer service. He began small, making sure he responded to every customer inquiry personally and within an hour. Over time, his customer base started to grow, slowly at first, but the impact was real.
Instead of trying to overhaul his entire business overnight, Sam made incremental changes. He improved his product by just 1% every month and increased his marketing reach little by little. These small improvements seemed minor at first, but they began to compound. Two years later, his business had tripled in revenue. What felt like insignificant actions had turned into massive growth. His secret? Compound growth— small, consistent actions that built upon each other over time.

Sam's story illustrates the importance of perseverance. You won't see dramatic changes right away, but the long-term payoff is worth the wait. Patience and consistency are your greatest allies when it comes to compounding progress.

Just like in personal development, compound growth plays a critical role in financial success. The legendary investor Warren Buffett is often celebrated for his mastery of this principle. Buffett didn't amass his billions by chasing quick wins; he started early, made smart, long-term investments, and allowed his wealth to grow exponentially through the power of compounding.

At the age of 11, Buffett bought his first shares of stock. He didn't try to flip them for a quick profit. Instead, he held onto them, reinvesting his earnings and allowing his money to compound over time. One of his most famous investments was his purchase of The Washington Post in the early 1970s. When Buffett invested, the stock was undervalued, but he had the patience to hold onto it, letting compound growth do the heavy lifting. Decades later, the value of his investment skyrocketed, contributing to his incredible fortune.

The lesson from Buffett and from Sam's story is simple: don't underestimate the power of small, consistent actions. Whether you're improving yourself or building wealth, success is rarely immediate. But when you commit to steady growth, even small changes can lead to extraordinary outcomes over time.

To fully harness the power of compound growth, here's what you need to do:

1. **Start Small**: Focus on small, positive actions that you can repeat consistently, whether it's in your finances, career, or personal life.
2. **Be Patient**: The results won't come overnight. Trust the process and stay committed, knowing that compound growth takes time.
3. **Track Your Progress**: Keep an eye on your incremental improvements. Celebrate small wins, because they are the building blocks of your future success.

By embracing the principle of compound growth, you can achieve lasting success in any area of your life. The power lies not in giant leaps, but in steady, consistent steps forward. Just like a snowball gathering momentum, your efforts will multiply, and in time, lead to significant transformation.
Once Again...

NEVER UNDERESTIMATE THE POWER OF COMPOUND GROWTH.

Law Thirty-six

Make Bad Habits Painful

"People do not change their behavior unless it makes them uncomfortable." — Dr. Phil McGraw

D ave Ramsey, a personal finance expert and radio host, offers a compelling example of making bad habits painful as a strategy for change. Ramsey's personal experience with financial struggles and his subsequent approach to overcoming them illustrate how attaching pain to negative behaviors can drive transformation.

In the early 1990s, Ramsey faced severe financial difficulties, including significant debt and bankruptcy. He realized that his approach to managing money was flawed and that he needed to make his bad financial habits painful to drive change. He took drastic measures to confront his financial issues head-on.

Ramsey created a detailed plan to address his debt, which included cutting unnecessary expenses, selling assets, and using the "snowball method" to pay off debts. He made the consequences of his financial mismanagement highly visible and emotionally impactful. By attaching pain to his bad financial habits, such as the stress and discomfort of living with debt, he motivated himself to stick to his plan.

Ramsey's experience underscores the effectiveness of making bad habits painful. By confronting the discomfort associated with negative behaviors and making significant changes, he was able to achieve financial stability and build a successful career as a financial advisor. His approach highlights the power of creating emotional and practical consequences to drive behavior change.

Making bad habits painful involves creating emotional or practical consequences that make negative behaviors less appealing. You can increase your motivation to change by attaching discomfort or inconvenience to undesirable habits.

Identify the negative behaviors you want to address and consider ways to make them more painful or uncomfortable. This could involve setting up consequences for not following through on your goals, such as financial penalties or social accountability.

Implement strategies to make the consequences of bad habits more immediate and impactful. For example, if you want to reduce procrastination, you might set strict deadlines and hold yourself accountable for missing them.

Use the discomfort associated with bad habits as a motivator for change. Embrace the pain as a signal that it is time to make positive adjustments. By creating a clear association between negative behaviors and their consequences, you can drive yourself to adopt healthier habits and achieve your goals.

Once Again...

MAKE BAD HABITS
- PAINFUL.-

Law Thirty-seven

Reward Yourself Along the Way

"Celebrate what you have accomplished, but raise the bar a little higher each time you succeed." — Mia Hamm

Marie Kondo, the renowned tidying expert and author of "The Life-Changing Magic of Tidying Up", demonstrates the importance of rewarding yourself along the way. Her approach to decluttering and organizing highlights how celebrating milestones can enhance motivation and reinforce positive behaviors.

Kondo's method involves decluttering by category and using the "KonMari" approach to assess each item's value. Throughout her decluttering journey, Kondo encouraged individuals to celebrate small victories and acknowledge the progress made. For example, she suggested that people take time to appreciate their achievements, such as completing a specific category or creating a more organized space.

By celebrating these milestones, individuals were able to maintain motivation and stay committed to the process. Kondo's approach emphasized that recognizing and rewarding progress, no matter how small, can help sustain enthusiasm and commitment to long-term goals.

Kondo's success as a tidying expert is a testament to the power of rewarding yourself along the way. Her method of celebrating milestones and acknowledging progress helped people transform their living spaces and maintain a positive mindset throughout the decluttering process.

Rewarding yourself along the way involves acknowledging and celebrating your achievements as you work toward your goals. This practice helps reinforce positive behaviors and maintain motivation, making it easier to stay committed to your objectives.

Set clear milestones and establish rewards for reaching them. For instance, if you are working on a fitness goal, reward yourself with a special treat or an enjoyable activity after reaching a milestone, such as completing a month of consistent workouts.

Choose rewards that are meaningful and align with your values. The rewards should enhance your sense of accomplishment and reinforce your commitment to your goals. Ensure that the rewards are attainable and proportionate to the effort required.

Regularly review your progress and celebrate both major and

minor milestones. Recognize the effort and dedication that contributed to your achievements and use these celebrations as motivation to continue striving toward your goals. By rewarding yourself along the way, you create a positive and reinforcing cycle that supports long-term success.

Once again...

REWARD YOURSELF

ALONG THE WAY.

Law Thirty-eight

Anchor Habits to Deep Purpose

"Without a sense of purpose, no matter what you accomplish, you will always feel unfulfilled." — *Anonymous*

Anchoring your habits to a deep sense of purpose involves connecting your daily actions to a meaningful goal or mission. When your habits are aligned with a greater purpose, you can maintain motivation and overcome challenges more effectively.

Start by identifying your core values and long-term goals. Reflect on what drives you and what you want to achieve in your life. This could be a personal mission, a professional ambition, or a cause you are passionate about.

Integrate your purpose into your daily habits and routines. Ensure that your actions are consistent with your goals and values. For example, if your purpose is to contribute to environmental sustainability, incorporate eco-friendly practices into your daily life.

Regularly revisit your purpose and assess how your habits align with it. Make adjustments as needed to ensure that your daily actions continue to support your mission. By anchoring your habits to a deep sense of purpose, you create a compelling reason to stay committed and motivated.

Elon Musk, the CEO of SpaceX and Tesla, is a prime example of anchoring habits to a deep sense of purpose. Musk's ventures are driven by his profound commitment to solving humanity's most pressing challenges, from sustainable energy to space exploration.

Musk's purpose is evident in his ambitious goals. At SpaceX, his mission is to make space travel more affordable and ultimately enable human life on Mars. At Tesla, his aim is to accelerate the world's transition to sustainable energy. This overarching sense of purpose anchors his daily habits and decisions, driving him to work long hours and tackle immense challenges.

One notable instance of Musk's purpose-driven approach is his work ethic. Despite facing numerous setbacks, including production delays and financial challenges, Musk's commitment to his vision keeps him motivated. His daily routines are structured around his goals, including spending significant time on product design and engineering.

Musk's story demonstrates the power of anchoring your habits to a deep sense of purpose. By aligning your daily actions with a meaningful mission, you can sustain motivation, overcome

obstacles, and achieve extraordinary results. Purpose serves as a driving force that fuels perseverance and commitment.
Once Again...

ANCHOR HABITS
TO DEEP PURPOSE.

Law Thirty-nine

Embrace the Plateau of Latent Potential

"The greatest oak was once a little nut who held its ground." — Anonymous

Embracing the plateau of latent potential involves understanding that progress may not always be immediately visible. There are periods of slow growth and seemingly stagnant phases that are a natural part of the process.

During these plateaus, focus on maintaining consistency and continuing your efforts. Recognize that growth and breakthroughs often occur after periods of persistence and hard work. Use these times as opportunities to refine your skills, strengthen your commitment, and stay focused on your goals.

Be patient and trust in the process. Understand that success may come gradually, and the results of your efforts may take time to manifest. Celebrate small victories and milestones along the way to maintain motivation and reinforce your commitment.

By embracing the plateau of latent potential, you can navigate the slower phases of progress with resilience and determination. Keep your long-term vision in mind and continue working toward your goals, knowing that sustained effort will eventually lead to significant breakthroughs.

J.K. Rowling's journey to success with Harry Potter is a powerful example of embracing the plateau of latent potential. Before becoming one of the best-selling authors of all time, Rowling faced numerous rejections and setbacks.

Rowling began writing the "Harry Potter" series while living as a single mother on welfare. The early stages of her writing career were marked by struggle and doubt. Her manuscript for the first book was rejected by multiple publishers. Despite these setbacks, Rowling persisted and continued to develop her story.

Eventually, her perseverance paid off. Bloomsbury Publishing agreed to publish Harry Potter and the Philosopher's Stone, and the book quickly gained popularity. The series went on to become a global phenomenon, making Rowling one of the most successful authors in history.

Rowling's story exemplifies the importance of embracing the plateau of latent potential. During the periods of struggle and slow progress, she remained committed to her goal and continued working toward her vision. Her eventual success underscores the value of persistence and faith in the long-term potential of her efforts.

Law Forty

Master One Habit to Master Them All

"Success is the sum of small efforts, repeated day in and day out." — *Robert Collier*

Mastering one habit involves focusing on a single, key behavior that can serve as a foundation for broader success. By dedicating your efforts to mastering one habit, you build the skills and discipline needed to tackle other areas of your life effectively.

Identify a habit that aligns with your long-term goals and has the potential to impact multiple aspects of your life. For example, if your goal is to improve overall productivity, start by mastering the habit of time management. This habit can enhance your efficiency and effectiveness in various areas.

Commit to consistently practicing and refining this habit. Track your progress, set specific goals, and make adjustments as needed. Use the skills and discipline gained from mastering one habit to build and develop other habits that support your overall objectives.

Celebrate your achievements and recognize the impact of mastering one habit on your broader success. By focusing on a single key behavior, you create a strong foundation for personal growth and unlock the potential to achieve your long-term goals.

Tony Robbins, the renowned life coach and motivational speaker, exemplifies the concept of mastering one habit to achieve broader success. Robbins' approach to personal development and his career trajectory illustrate how focusing on one habit can create a foundation for mastering other areas of life.

In the early stages of his career, Robbins focused on mastering the habit of public speaking. He dedicated significant time to honing his speaking skills, delivering seminars, and building his presence as a motivational speaker. This single habit of mastering public speaking became the cornerstone of his career.

Robbins' commitment to this habit opened doors to new opportunities. As he gained expertise in public speaking, he expanded his influence and developed additional habits related to personal growth and business success. His focus on mastering one key habit provided him with the platform to build and refine other skills.

Today, Robbins' career is a testament to the power of mastering one habit. His success in public speaking laid the groundwork for his achievements in writing, coaching, and entrepreneurship. Robbins' story demonstrates that mastering one habit can serve as a catalyst for broader success and personal development.

Law Forty-one

Design Your Default Actions

"Success is the sum of small efforts, repeated day in and day out." — Robert Collier

Tim Ferriss, the author of The 4-Hour Workweek, offers a compelling example of designing default actions to enhance productivity. Ferriss's approach to optimizing work and life through automation and strategic defaults demonstrates how setting up your environment can lead to more effective habits.

In his quest to achieve a more productive lifestyle, Ferriss implemented the concept of designing default actions. He focused on creating systems and routines that made it easier to perform desired actions automatically, rather than relying on willpower alone.

For instance, Ferriss implemented the "batch processing" approach to manage his tasks. Instead of handling emails and small tasks throughout the day, he designated specific times for these activities, reducing decision fatigue and increasing efficiency. By setting clear defaults for when and how tasks should be completed, Ferriss streamlined his workflow and freed up time for more meaningful activities.

Another example of Ferriss's default action design is his use of automation tools. He set up systems to automate routine tasks, such as scheduling social media posts and managing finances. These defaults allowed him to focus on high-impact activities and maintain a more balanced work-life schedule.

Ferriss's productivity revolution illustrates the power of designing default actions. By creating systems and routines that make desired behaviors automatic, you can enhance efficiency, reduce decision fatigue, and achieve your goals more effectively.

Designing your default actions involves creating systems and routines that make it easier to engage in positive behaviors without relying on constant willpower. You can achieve greater consistency and efficiency by setting up your environment and routines to support your goals.

Start by identifying the key behaviors or tasks you want to automate. Consider how you can structure your environment to support these behaviors. For example, if you want to develop a habit of exercising regularly, place your workout clothes and gear in a visible and accessible location.

Establish clear routines and systems that support your goals. Schedule specific times for tasks, set up automated reminders, and use tools that streamline your workflow. By creating default actions that align with your objectives, you reduce the need for constant decision-making and make positive behaviors more automatic.

Regularly evaluate and adjust your default actions as needed. Ensure that your routines and systems continue to support your goals and make adjustments to improve efficiency. By designing your default actions, you create a supportive environment that fosters consistency and success.

Law Forty-two

Integrate Rest into Your Routine

"Almost everything will work again if you unplug it for a few minutes, including you." — Anne Lamott

Integrating rest into your routine is essential for maintaining long-term productivity and well-being. Rest and recovery are crucial components of a balanced lifestyle and play a significant role in achieving sustained success.

Start by evaluating your current routine and identifying areas where you can incorporate rest and recovery. Prioritize getting sufficient sleep each night, and create a relaxing bedtime routine to improve sleep quality. Ensure that you allocate time for breaks and relaxation throughout the day to avoid burnout.

Incorporate activities that promote relaxation and rejuvenation, such as meditation, stretching, or leisure activities. Schedule regular periods of downtime and ensure that you disconnect from work and digital devices to recharge.

Recognize the signs of fatigue and listen to your body's need for rest. Make adjustments to your routine as needed to maintain a healthy balance between work and rest. By integrating rest into your daily habits, you enhance your overall well-being and sustain your ability to achieve long-term goals.

Arianna Huffington, the founder of The Huffington Post and author of The Sleep Revolution, experienced a profound personal transformation after collapsing from exhaustion in 2007. This pivotal moment led her to reevaluate her approach to work and rest, ultimately reshaping her understanding of productivity and well-being.

Huffington's collapse was a wake-up call that highlighted the importance of rest and recovery. She realized that her relentless work schedule and lack of sleep were detrimental to her health and performance. This experience prompted her to explore the science of sleep and the role of rest in achieving long-term success.

In her book The Sleep Revolution, Huffington advocates for integrating rest and recovery into daily routines. She emphasizes the benefits of quality sleep, taking breaks, and prioritizing self-care. Huffington's approach involves creating a balanced routine that includes adequate sleep, relaxation, and time for rejuvenation.

Huffington's story exemplifies the significance of integrating rest into your routine. By prioritizing rest and self-care, she was able to enhance her overall well-being and performance. Her journey underscores the value of recognizing the importance of rest and incorporating it into your daily habits.

Once Again...

INTEGRATE REST INTO YOUR ROUTINE

Use Visual Cues to Solidify Habits

"Visualize your highest self and start showing up as that person." — Unknown

Marie Kondo, the celebrated tidying expert and author of The Life-Changing Magic of Tidying Up, demonstrates the power of visual cues in building and maintaining habits. Kondo's method of using visual cues to organize and declutter is a testament to how visual reminders can support habit formation and behavior change.

Kondo's KonMari method involves visualizing an organized space and using visual cues to maintain order. For example, she suggests arranging items in a way that makes them visible and accessible, creating a visually appealing and functional environment. This approach helps individuals maintain organization and reduce clutter over time.

One practical application of Kondo's method is the use of clear storage containers and labeled bins. By making items easily visible and accessible, individuals are more likely to adhere to organizational habits and maintain a tidy space. Visual cues serve as constant reminders of the desired behavior and help reinforce positive habits.

Kondo's success highlights the effectiveness of using visual cues to solidify habits. By incorporating visual reminders and organizing your environment to support your goals, you can enhance your ability to maintain positive behaviors and achieve long-term success.

Using visual cues to solidify habits involves incorporating reminders and signals into your environment that support your desired behaviors. Visual cues can serve as powerful tools to reinforce positive habits and keep you focused on your goals.

Start by identifying key behaviors you want to reinforce and consider how visual cues can support these habits. For example, if you are working on a fitness goal, place workout gear in a visible location to remind you to exercise regularly.

Create visual reminders that align with your goals and integrate them into your daily environment. Use charts, notes, or images to track progress and reinforce positive behaviors. Ensure that these visual cues are easily accessible and regularly visible to maintain motivation.

Regularly update and adjust your visual cues as needed to keep them relevant and effective. By incorporating visual reminders into your routine, you create a supportive environment that enhances your ability to maintain habits and achieve your objectives.

Law Forty-four

Build Flexibility into Your Habits

"Flexibility is the key to stability." — *John Wooden*

uilding flexibility into your habits involves creating routines and strategies that can adapt to changing circumstances and new information. Flexibility allows you to respond effectively to unexpected challenges and opportunities, maintaining progress toward your goals.

Start by evaluating your current habits and routines. Identify areas where rigidity might hinder your ability to adapt to new situations. For example, if you have a strict workout schedule that doesn't accommodate unexpected changes, consider building flexibility into your fitness routine.

Incorporate adaptable strategies into your habits. For instance, if you are working on improving your productivity, use a flexible planning system that allows for adjustments based on changing priorities. Techniques such as time blocking with buffer periods or dynamic to-do lists can help accommodate shifts in your schedule.

Regularly review and adjust your habits to ensure they remain effective in the face of change. Stay open to experimenting with new approaches and be willing to modify your routines as needed. By building flexibility into your habits, you enhance your ability to adapt and thrive in a dynamic environment.

Jeff Bezos, the founder of Amazon, is a prime example of how building flexibility into habits can lead to remarkable success. Bezos's approach to business and innovation underscores the importance of adaptability in achieving long-term goals.

In the early days of Amazon, Bezos was known for his relentless focus on customer satisfaction and continuous improvement. As the e-commerce landscape evolved, Bezos demonstrated remarkable flexibility by adapting Amazon's business model and operations to changing market conditions.

One significant instance of Bezos's flexibility was Amazon's transition from a bookstore to a comprehensive online retailer. Recognizing the potential of expanding beyond books, Bezos adapted Amazon's offerings to include a wide range of products, from electronics to groceries. This shift not only broadened Amazon's market reach but also solidified its position as a leading global retailer.

Bezos also embraced flexibility in Amazon's operational strategies. The company's use of data analytics and customer feedback allowed it to continuously refine its services and adapt to emerging trends. For example, the introduction of Amazon Prime was a response to customer demands for faster shipping and exclusive benefits.

Bezos's story illustrates the value of building flexibility into your habits and strategies. By being open to change and willing to adapt, you can navigate challenges and seize new opportunities, ensuring long-term success and resilience.

Law Forty-five

Never Neglect Reflection

"Reflection is the lamp that illuminates the path ahead." — Anonymous

Oprah Winfrey, the media mogul and philanthropist, exemplifies the power of reflection in personal and professional growth. Winfrey's career is marked by her commitment to self-reflection and continuous improvement, which has played a significant role in her success.

Throughout her career, Winfrey has emphasized the

importance of reflection in her personal and professional life. She often speaks about her practice of journaling and introspection as tools for self-discovery and growth. This reflective practice has helped her navigate challenges, set new goals, and maintain a clear sense of purpose.

One notable instance of Winfrey's reflective approach was her decision to launch *The Oprah Winfrey Show* in 1986. Reflecting on her earlier experiences in television and her desire to create meaningful content, Winfrey focused the show on personal growth, inspiration, and human connection. This reflective insight shaped the show's format and contributed to its immense success.

Winfrey's reflective practices extend to her philanthropic efforts as well. She frequently evaluates the impact of her charitable work and adjusts her approach based on feedback and outcomes. This commitment to reflection ensures that her initiatives remain effective and aligned with her values.

Winfrey's story demonstrates the value of never neglecting reflection. You can enhance your growth and achieve long-term success by regularly assessing your progress, learning from experiences, and adjusting your strategies.

Never neglecting reflection involves regularly evaluating your progress, learning from experiences, and making adjustments to your strategies. Reflection provides valuable insights that can guide your decision-making and help you stay aligned with your goals.

Incorporate regular reflection into your routine. Set aside time each week or month to review your progress, assess your achievements, and identify areas for improvement. Use this time to reflect on your successes, challenges, and lessons learned.

Utilize various reflective practices, such as journaling, meditation, or discussing your experiences with a mentor or coach. These practices can help you gain clarity, set new goals, and refine your strategies.

Be open to feedback and willing to make adjustments based on your reflections. Recognize that reflection is an ongoing process that can provide valuable insights for continuous improvement. By never neglecting reflection, you enhance your ability to navigate challenges, seize opportunities, and achieve your long-term objectives.

Law Forty-six

Use Peer Pressure as a Force for Good

"You are the average of the five people you spend the most time with." — Jim Rohn

Eric Ries, the author of The Lean Startup, successfully leveraged peer pressure to drive innovation and entrepreneurship through his Lean Startup methodology. The Lean Startup community exemplifies how peer influence can be harnessed for positive outcomes and personal growth.

Ries's Lean Startup methodology emphasizes the importance

of validating ideas through experimentation, learning from failures, and iterating quickly. This approach has gained widespread adoption among entrepreneurs and startups, creating a supportive community focused on continuous improvement and innovation.

One example of this positive peer pressure is the Lean Startup conferences and meetups, where entrepreneurs gather to share their experiences, learn from each other, and support one another's growth. These events create an environment of accountability and motivation, encouraging participants to adopt best practices and pursue their goals with greater determination.

The Lean Startup community also leverages peer pressure through mentorship and networking. Experienced entrepreneurs and industry experts offer guidance and support to newcomers, creating a culture of collaboration and mutual growth. This peer influence fosters a sense of accountability and encourages individuals to strive for excellence and innovation.

Ries's use of peer pressure as a force for good highlights the power of surrounding yourself with supportive and like-minded individuals. By leveraging positive peer influence, you can enhance your motivation, gain valuable insights, and achieve your goals more effectively.

Using peer pressure as a force for good involves leveraging the influence of your social circle to support and reinforce positive behaviors and goals. Surrounding yourself with individuals who share your values and aspirations can enhance your motivation and drive.

Start by evaluating your current social circle and identifying individuals who align with your goals and values. Seek out communities, groups, or networks that foster positive behaviors and provide support for your objectives.

Engage with these communities and build relationships with individuals who can offer encouragement, accountability, and guidance. Participate in events, discussions, and activities that reinforce your goals and provide opportunities for learning and growth.

Utilize peer pressure as a tool for accountability. Share your goals with your social circle and seek feedback and support. By creating a network of positive influences, you can enhance your motivation, stay focused on your objectives, and achieve your goals more effectively.

Regularly assess the impact of your social circle on your progress and make adjustments as needed. Surround yourself with individuals who inspire and challenge you, and continue to leverage peer pressure as a force for good in your personal and professional growth.

Law Forty-seven

Replace, do not Erase

"Habits are not a finish line to be crossed, they are a lifestyle to be lived." — James Clear

Replacing habits involves shifting your focus from trying to erase negative behaviors to replacing them with positive alternatives. You can effectively manage and overcome detrimental patterns by redirecting your energy toward constructive habits.

Start by identifying the negative habits you want to change. Instead of solely focusing on eliminating these habits, consider what positive behaviors you can introduce to replace them. For example, if you are trying to cut down on unhealthy snacking, replace it with a habit of eating fresh fruits or nuts.

Create a plan to incorporate the new, positive habit into your daily routine. Ensure that this habit is specific, achievable, and aligned with your goals. Utilize tools such as habit-tracking apps or visual reminders to reinforce the new behavior and monitor your progress.

Gradually phase out the old habit by replacing it with the new one. The key is to focus on building consistency with the positive habit while reducing the frequency of the negative one. Over time, the new behavior will become more ingrained, and the old habit will lose its hold.

Regularly review your progress and make adjustments as needed. Celebrate your successes and remain committed to the new habit. By focusing on replacing rather than erasing, you can create lasting change and achieve your desired outcomes.

Jerry Seinfeld, the iconic comedian known for his successful TV show Seinfeld, provides a remarkable example of replacing habits rather than trying to erase them. Seinfeld's method for maintaining productivity and creativity is an insightful demonstration of how to replace old habits with new, positive ones.

In the early 2000s, Seinfeld was grappling with the challenge of staying productive and creative while juggling his busy schedule. His solution came in the form of a unique habit-stacking method, which he famously described as the "Seinfeld Strategy." This method involved replacing unproductive habits with a consistent, daily routine that prioritized creativity and writing.

Seinfeld's approach was simple yet effective. He set a goal to write new material every day and marked each completed day on a calendar with a big red X. This visual representation of his progress became a powerful motivator. Each day he completed his writing task, he added an X to the calendar, creating a visual chain of success. The longer the chain grew, the more motivated Seinfeld was to continue his writing habit.

Instead of trying to erase procrastination or distractions, Seinfeld focused on replacing them with a positive, reinforcing habit. By creating a visual system that celebrated daily progress, he turned habit formation into a rewarding and motivating process.

Seinfeld's success with the Seinfeld Strategy highlights the effectiveness of replacing old habits with new, positive ones. Rather than focusing on eliminating negative behaviors, his approach involved redirecting his energy toward a constructive routine that reinforced his goals and fostered consistent progress.

Once Again...

REPLACE,
DON'T ERASE.

Law Forty-eight

Let Your Habits Evolve

"Change is the only constant in life." — Heraclitus

L etting your habits evolve involves recognizing that change is a natural and necessary part of personal and professional growth. As your goals and circumstances evolve, so should your habits and routines.

Start by assessing your current habits and evaluating their effectiveness in achieving your goals. Identify areas where adjustments or improvements are needed to better align with your evolving objectives.

Be open to experimenting with new approaches and strategies. Allow yourself the flexibility to adapt your habits based on changing circumstances, feedback, and new insights. Embrace the process of continuous improvement and remain willing to refine your habits as needed.

Regularly review your progress and assess how well your evolving habits are supporting your goals. Make adjustments and fine-tune your routines to ensure they remain effective and aligned with your objectives. By letting your habits evolve, you create a dynamic and responsive approach to personal growth and achievement.

Elon Musk, the visionary entrepreneur behind companies like Tesla and SpaceX, exemplifies the concept of allowing habits to evolve as part of a broader journey of innovation and growth. Musk's ability to adapt and refine his habits and strategies has played a crucial role in his success across various industries.

One notable example of Musk's evolving habits is his approach to time management and productivity. Early in his career, Musk was known for working long hours and maintaining a demanding schedule. However, as his ventures grew in complexity, he recognized the need to adapt his habits to effectively manage his time and energy.

Musk's solution involved a strategic approach to time blocking and prioritization. He developed a method for scheduling his day in five-minute blocks, allowing him to focus intensely on specific tasks while maximizing productivity. This evolving habit enabled him to manage multiple high-stakes projects simultaneously and make significant progress across his various ventures.

Another example of Musk's adaptability is his approach to leadership and team management. As Tesla and SpaceX expanded, Musk adapted his leadership style to foster innovation and collaboration. He implemented new practices to encourage creativity, such as open communication and a culture of experimentation. These evolving habits have helped drive the success of his companies and push the boundaries of technological advancements.

Musk's story illustrates the importance of allowing your habits to evolve in response to changing circumstances and goals. By continuously adapting and refining your habits, you can stay aligned with your objectives and drive progress in your personal and professional life.

And finally…

LET YOUR HABIT EVOLVE.

About the Author

Victor O. Carl is the pen name of a visionary researcher and author whose mission is to empower individuals to unlock their full potential. With a background rooted in extensive research and a passion for personal growth, Carl has authored several transformative books.

His first book, *The 48 Laws of Mental Power*, takes readers deep into the unseen forces driving human behavior, unlocking strategies to sharpen the mind and fortify inner resilience. Carl continued his quest for self-mastery in *The 48 Laws of Habit Mastery*, delivering timeless methods to transform routines and habits into tools of success. With *The 48 Laws of Money*, Carl demystifies the secrets of wealth-building, bridging psychology and financial wisdom, while *The 48 Laws of Peace* offers readers a path to inner tranquility in an increasingly chaotic world.

Carl's books are not just guides but manuals for survival in a world designed to overwhelm the individual. Drawing from his profound experiences and deep research, he challenges readers to transcend the limitations imposed by society and their own conditioning. His work is crafted for those who are ready to break free, master themselves, and achieve lasting transformation. You can Visit his website below For Updates.

www.48lol.com

Acknowledgments

I am deeply grateful to my family, especially my wife and kids (Videl, Vishal, and Valen), and to my friends for their unwavering support and belief in my vision. To the mentors and thinkers whose ideas shaped these works—thank you for your invaluable guidance.

A heartfelt thanks to my readers, whose curiosity and dedication to personal growth inspire me to continue writing. These books are for all who seek mastery over their minds, habits, and lives.

Thank you for being part of this journey.